Edible
Art

Forty-eight
Garnishes
for the
Professional

EDIBLE
ART

David
Paul
Larousse

CBI

A CBI Book
Published by Van Nostrand Reinhold Company
New York

To the artist
inside every chef,
cook, and cuisinier,
hidden or flourishing.

A CBI BOOK
(CBI is an imprint of Van Nostrand Reinhold Company Inc.)
Copyright © 1987 by Van Nostrand Reinhold Company Inc.
Library of Congress Catalog Card Number 86-9226
ISBN 0-442-25832-1

Printed in the United States of America

Designed by Charlotte Staub

All line illustrations by David Paul Larousse

All photographs, except as otherwise noted, by Constance Brown

Published by Van Nostrand Reinhold Company Inc.
115 Fifth Avenue
New York, New York 10003

Van Nostrand Reinhold Company Limited
Molly Millars Lane
Wokingham, Berkshire RG11 2PY, England

Van Nostrand Reinhold
480 LaTrobe Street
Melbourne, Victoria 3000, Australia

Macmillan of Canada
Division of Canada Publishing Corporation
164 Commander Boulevard
Agincourt, Ontario M1S 3C7, Canada

16 15 14 13 12 11 10 9 8 7 6 5 4 3 2

Library of Congress Cataloging-in-Publication Data

Larousse, David Paul, 1949–
    Edible art.

    "A CBI book."
    Includes index.
    1. Cookery (Garnishes)   I. Title.
TX652.L337 1986   641.5   86-9226
ISBN 0-442-25832-1

CONTENTS

ACKNOWLEDGMENTS

I wish to thank the following individuals for their significant contributions to the completion of this book: Phil Mason, who personally delivered my proposal to the publisher; Jeanette Mall, my editor, for being patient and professional throughout; Chef-Instructor Ben Quicho, Johnson & Wales Culinary School, for sharing his exquisite sculptured roses; Chef Alan Gibson, of the Ritz Carlton, Washington, D.C., for his selfless support and endless encouragement; and Susan E. Mitchell, for her assistance with, and general support in, my preparation of the illustrations. Without their help, this book could not have been completed.

PREFACE

Of all the classes that I took at my alma mater, the Culinary Institute of America (CIA), the two I enjoyed most were *garde-manger* and buffet catering. In *garde-manger*, we were introduced to the nuts and bolts of food decoration. In buffet catering, we began to assemble our decorated handiwork into full-scale buffets.

The *garde-manger* is the cold kitchen, the department that produces decorated food. Under this heading come all types of cold meat, fish, fruit, and cheese platters, all varieties of salads, hors d'oeuvre and canapés, pâtés, galantines, terrines, chaud-froid centerpieces, tallow and butter sculptures, ice carvings, and sorbets.

The *garde-manger* allows the chef's artistic talents to flourish. During the fifteen years that I have been working in the culinary field, I have encountered some phenomenally talented individuals, and I have been amazed by the beauty, simplicity, and aesthetic nature of their decorative work. Over the years, I, too, have built up a repertoire of garnishes and decorative techniques, both the traditional variety and ones that are uniquely mine.

The artist in me thrived on those classes many years ago. I was drawn to the visual excitement that can enhance the dining experience. It seemed to me that culinary art was as valid as any other art form, so I set out to investigate that idea, to confirm my theory.

Culinary art is perhaps even more profound an art form than drawing, painting, sculpture, ballet, or opera. A drawing or painting is seen, an opera seen and heard, a sculpture seen and touched, a symphony heard. Culinary art is perceived very differently. The viewer—or, should I say, the diner—not only sees the artful creation, he also smells it, tastes it, feels its texture, and in some cases hears it (as with a sizzling steak or a bubbling fondue). All five senses are involved in the act of eating. What more comprehensive sensory experience can there be? Shouldn't this ensure its proper place among the great arts of humankind?

9

The primary difference between recognized art pursuits and the culinary arts is the ultimate destiny of the medium. The "art" produced in a kitchen is the most transient of any. Within a few days, and sometimes only a few hours, every culinary creation falls under the scrutiny of a hungry individual, who, with tools in hand, proceeds to demolish the "art." No other art undergoes such a transformation. True, symphonies, operas, and ballets are transient, even abstract, in nature. But these performing arts are now preserved on tape, record, or video, and then enjoyed over and over again in that form. Drawings, paintings, and sculptures may last for centuries. Culinary art, on the other hand, is never savored again.

Recognizing this transience, and finding a way to accommodate it, was a significant step in the development of my culinary skills and in my search for the art in food. Although I had had no formal artistic training before enrolling in the CIA, I nonetheless considered myself an artist, having won several awards in drawing competitions in my public school days. Both of my parents were freelance commercial artists, which also may have contributed to that perception. Since I saw myself as an artist, and most artists look forward to enjoying their creations over and over again, the total destruction of each creative work threatened to foster an eternal dilemma. Imagine each magnificent buffet platter, every entrée, soufflé, torte, tart, and pâté—each one an intensely beautiful picture, a harmonious blend of texture, color, bouquet, and taste painstakingly created by the chef-artiste—suddenly gone forever. Imagine each labor of love destined to disappear, with no chance for future appreciation.

Before I could continue my pursuit of the "art" in culinary arts, I had to resolve this dilemma. I had to protect myself from the danger of becoming emotionally drained and depressed by the transience of the food medium. My solution was twofold. First, I cultivated a detachment from my finished work. Just as with a one-night stand, a family member who passes away, or a sibling who grows up and moves away, I am intimately connected to my work until its completion—then we go our separate ways. On to bigger and better things for both of us. When my work leaves the kitchen, I have finished. I put it out of my mind and turn my attention to other works, other menus, other kitchen-related duties.

Second, I do not make the assumption that I always will receive positive feedback as a result of my work. I decided that any accolades would be icing on the cake, a bonus. And that bonus—the word of gratitude, the invitation to join a table of guests for an after-dinner cordial—is sufficient feedback to keep my creative fires burning. And it is that much more satisfying if it is unexpected.

Thus, I decided to think of myself as an invisible wizard, one who could thrill the eyes, ears, nose, hands, and heart of an unsuspecting recipient, inside of whom my handiwork would be transformed into new flesh, blood, and body cells. If the power and seduction of my efforts were successful, then that brief event in the life of the diner would be a memorable one. That meal could well lift the spirits and soothe the troubled heart of a recipient. All this, at least, projected some solace into my oh-so-fragile art. Exploring this transience, and discovering a way to shield myself from the hazards inherent in that transience, also helped shape my conclusion about the "art" in culinary arts.

Art must come to fruition for art's sake alone. The artist seeks to express some part of his emotional self through his work. Those who see his work will feel that emotional message, which will in turn ignite emotional responses in them. There is no need to be a painter, sculptor, singer, or dancer in order to be moved by a powerful drawing, a heartrending song, or a classical ballet. But my *Boeuf braisé à la mode Parisienne, avec Pommes risolées*—as magnificent as it may be—can be only meat and potatoes to a hungry restaurant patron. Where is the art when someone is hungry and just wants a plate of hot food?

Thus, after fifteen years of plying this trade, and of considering the question "Is it art?", I have come to the conclusion that the chef—or, to sound even more professional, the cuisinier—is primarily a craftsperson. A carpenter can construct a wooden house frame with mathematical precision and exquisitely fashioned dovetailed joints, but the house frame is only a support structure destined to be covered by roofing and siding. The carpenter can be very artful in the way he assembles that house frame, and he can even

11

perceive himself as an artist, but his contribution, in the most basic sense, is shelter. Do the residents of that house think about the "art" in a part of it that they never see? In the same way, a chef or cuisinier, though perceiving himself or herself as an artist, may be only rarely appreciated as such. The chef remains a craftsperson, albeit at times a very artful one within that craft. But the transience of the medium and the basic need to consume food will always prevent a chef from attaining permanent and full-time status as an artist.

This book is an outgrowth of my search for the "art" in the culinary arts, and my passion for exposing my guests to the power, charm, and beauty that exist in food. As a working chef, I have used all of the garnishes described. All have been tested in the pressure-packed environment that often exists in the kitchen. This means that all can be produced within the rhythms of the kitchen in order to embellish a plate or platter of food and to make that presentation a pleasure to behold. That *people eat with their eyes first* is a significant axiom in this craft. The first glance at a plate of food initiates the flow of gastric juices and is an important prerequisite to the enjoyment of the dish. If it looks good, it usually follows that it will taste good.

The garnish elements in the projects that follow can also be assembled into grander and more sophisticated efforts, such as "California *mukimono,*" a name I have given to full bouquets assembled with dozens of individual vegetable flowers. (*Mukimono* is a Japanese word meaning "to slice things," and it refers to the Japanese food aesthetic. I added "California" because I was born in Southern California and have spent half of my years as a working chef in San Francisco.) Photographs of some of my California *mukimono* bouquets are included in the color section of this book. All were entries in professional culinary and food-sculpture competitions. At such events, professional chefs display their artistic skills, and I have seen some phenomenal works on these occasions. It is during these competitions that the culinary arts come closest to being art. But even then, the transience, the temporary status of food interferes with true artistic status.

12

I am well aware that when I achieve some measure of beauty in my work, and that work is applauded, then I have pushed the limits of craftsmanship toward art. But as a working chef, I am still a craftsman, thriving on the lift I get when all the components are just right—the ambience, the audience, and the food. At such a moment, my ego forces a slip of the tongue, and I inadvertently refer to my handiwork, my culinary craft, as "edible art."

A style note: While both men and women fill the ranks of fine professional chefs, it is far less cumbersome to use a single gender when discussing the craft. So, for simplicity's sake, all references that follow are masculine—with absolutely no intention of slighting the legions of competent female chefs.

TOOLS

Professional cooks have a tendency to accumulate a great many more tools, cutters, and gadgets than they ever will use on a regular basis. I know this is true because I have a tendency to do just that. There is always something appealing about buying the very latest gadget—even though that gadget may be beyond what the profession requires.

You can make all of the garnishes in this volume with two basic tools: a sharp paring knife and a sharp fillet knife. Then, to keep them sharp, you will need a sharpening stone and a steel. Additions to this repertoire of tools are included here as timesavers and as aids for novices in achieving uniformity. Even those who have a good grasp of all of the cutting techniques will find that using additional tools shortens production time while maintaining uniformity.

The list below is intended merely as a guide; it will vary from cook to cook, from menu to menu.

Paring Knife: This is the single most important tool in your carving repertoire. The blade, which should be roughly 3 inches long, comes in a variety of shapes. The most common blade shape is the same as that of a traditional French knife (see below), having a slightly beveled cutting edge. (Variations in blade shapes are shown in the accompanying photograph.)

Fillet Knife: The 6-inch-long blade of this knife is flexible enough to bend with the slightest pressure. It is used most often to remove a fish fillet from the bones and skin. Its flexibility is useful for hard-to-reach places when making garnishes.

Sharpening Stone: A sharpening stone is absolutely indispensable for making garnishes, since knife edges must be kept razor sharp. Carborundum stones (also called oilstones) come in a variety of sizes and shapes. The sharpening stone made by Ekco is a small, rectangular stone attached to a small piece of wood. It is the most efficient sharpening stone I have come across. Carborundum stones can be lubricated with either honing oil (a highly refined mineral oil) or water. I prefer water mixed with a few drops of lemon juice, because it works fine and is less messy than oil.

Sharpening Steel: This elongated, rough-textured tool is not exactly a sharpener, but it puts a sharp edge on any knife during its use, as well as between sharpenings with the stone. A half-dozen swipes of the blade along a steel removes the ultrafine burrs created during the knife's use. The tip of the shaft of a traditional steel is slightly magnetized, to attract those burrs. A newer version uses ceramic instead, which is smaller and lighter, and thus less cumbersome to carry, than a standard steel.

Below are listed a number of specialized cutting tools. Even though they are not essential, each has a purpose and use for creating appealing garnishes. Many are already part of the inventory in a well-stocked kitchen. (They are listed in alphabetical order, not in the order of their necessity.)

Bamboo Skewers and Paddle-Ended Toothpicks: Long bamboo skewers are used as supports for the staircase on page **87**. They can also be used for flower stems if you insert one in the underside of a flower and cover the skewer with the green tubular leaf of a scallion. Paddle-ended toothpicks are used as oars for the cucumber boat on page **75**.

Channel Knife: This tool cuts a uniform V-shaped channel into the surface of a fruit or vegetable. It is also referred to as a "stripper" because of the strip of vegetable or fruit that it removes. The strips can also be used for decorative effects.

Chinese Cleaver: This all-purpose, wide-bladed knife, which can be found in any Asian cutlery or hardware store, is relatively inexpensive. The blade has a slight curvature that allows you to rock it back and forth as you cut. Some of these cleavers are manufactured with a metal handle as an integral part of the blade. Others have wooden handles, but generally they are not of the same high quality as more expensive cutlery, and they tend to crack or split after several years of use. This is a very versatile tool, and in the hands of a skilled cuisinier, it has an infinite number of functions.

Chinese Flower Cutters: Four-cutter sets, available in two size ranges, are sold in most gourmet shops and many Asian grocery markets. With the help of these cutters, beautiful and uniform flowers can be cut out in seconds. The two sets pictured are marketed by

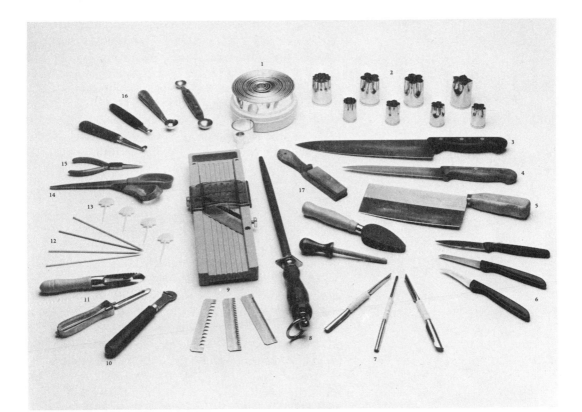

Garnishing Tools:
1. concentric circle cutters
2. Chinese flower cutters
3. French knife
4. fillet knife
5. Chinese cleaver
6. three paring knives
7. Chinese sculpting tools
8. full-length sharpening steel
9. Japanese *mandoline* and three blades
10. channel knife
11. vegetable peelers
12. bamboo skewers
13. plastic toothpicks
14. scissors
15. needlenose pliers
16. four Parisienne scoops, or melon ballers
17. three small ceramic sharpening steels

Joyce Chen, author of several books on Chinese cuisine.

Chinese Sculpting Tools: This trio of inexpensive U- and V-shaped sculpting tools can be found at Asian and gourmet markets. They are used to trim and peel certain hard-to-reach areas. They can also be used to cut U- and V-shaped grooves, producing more uniform cuts than those created with a paring knife and deeper cuts than those made with a channel knife.

Concentric Circle Cutters: These are helpful aids to cutting and scoring in perfect circles.

French Knife: This is the most frequently used knife in a professional cook's tool kit. It comes in a variety of blade lengths, from 6 to 14 inches. The blade has a slightly beveled cutting edge and an even more slightly beveled back edge: both edges intersect at the point of the blade. As a garnishing tool, it is used to cut large vegetables into small segments that will later be turned into finished garnishes.

17

Mandoline: There are two commonly available versions of this tool. One is a potato *mandoline*, a stainless-steel tool traditionally used to make several classical cuts of potatoes (*allumettes*/matchsticks, *frites*/ french fries, *gaufrettes*/waffles, *pailles*/straws, and chips). This professional tool can be fairly costly. The second variety, marketed by a Japanese manufacturer, is the Benriner Food Slicer, a practical and well-designed gadget made of hard plastic. It has a blade that is removable for sharpening and cleaning, and it comes with three additional cutting attachments for three different julienne sizes. The slicer is available at Asian markets and gourmet shops. You can use either one of these devices to create the uniform slices required for several of the garnishes.

If you use an electric slicer, either a home variety or the commercial version, *remember to use the hand guard at all times*!

Parisienne Scoop: Commonly referred to as a "melon baller," this marvelous gadget cuts little spheres out of any fruit or vegetable. (Any sauce or dish tagged with the name *Parisienne* will have some kind of spherically cut garnish on or in it.) The scoop is used to make the spherical indentations in a number of garnishes in this book. It is available in a variety of sizes, as large as 1 inch and as small as $3/16$ inch. (The smallest-size scoop is called a "pois," or pea scoop.) Some versions of this tool have a large scoop and a small scoop at opposite ends of the handle.

Scissors: A pair of lightweight stainless-steel scissors can come in handy for making zigzag patterns and for trimming and snipping on a wide array of projects.

Vegetable Peeler: Probably every kitchen in America has at least one of these devices. It is available in just about any grocery store and is very inexpensive. The trick with this tool is to know how to sharpen it. Sharpening a vegetable peeler properly will increase its life tenfold or more. Grasp the peeler in one hand and put the tip of the tool on a cutting board. Pick up a sharpening steel in the other hand and press the tip of the steel into the concave (hollow) side of the blade, at roughly a 30-degree angle. Keeping the tip of the steel pressed firmly into the peeler blade, run the steel back and forth the full length of the blade.

Part I | # BASIC FLOWER FORMS

Zucchini Crown

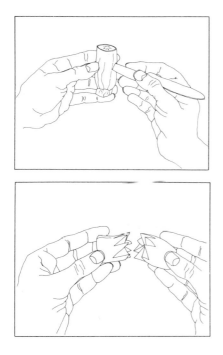

With a utility knife, cut a 3-inch-long segment from one end of a small to medium zucchini squash. Hold the zucchini segment, cut end up, in one hand. Grasp a paring knife between the thumb and forefinger of your other hand, perpendicular to the zucchini. Insert the knife at about the middle of the perimeter of the segment, into and just past the center of the squash. For this particular flower, the first cut is vertical, about ½ inch high.

Begin the second cut at the top of the first cut, with the knife still pointed toward the center of the squash, but turn the blade so that it is at a 45-degree angle to the first cut. The third cut, still directed toward the center, is again vertical. The fourth is turned slightly, the fifth vertical, and so on. Continue this zigzag pattern around the zucchini until the last angled cut finishes at the bottom of the original vertical cut. Be sure to insert the knife each time just slightly past the vertical center of the squash, so that the pieces will separate easily and cleanly.

Now separate the two parts gently. If you have any difficulty in doing this, reinsert the knife to make sure each incision intersects the previous one. Two zucchini crowns should remain.

This cutting technique is very basic, and you can apply it to almost any fruit or vegetable—onion, apple, tomato, radish, crookneck squash, melon, carrot, orange, lemon, or lime. Changes in height, angles, number of cuts, and the direction of the knife around the perimeter of the fruit or vegetable allow an infinite number of variations in this flower form. If a whole brigade of cooks went to work on zucchini crowns at the same time, following the same instructions, each crown would be different.

This garnish can be prepared in advance. It will store for up to three days if immersed in cold water and refrigerated. Change the water daily.

Use zucchini crowns as components in bouquets or assemble a small grouping of them to garnish individual plates.

Onion Chrysanthemum

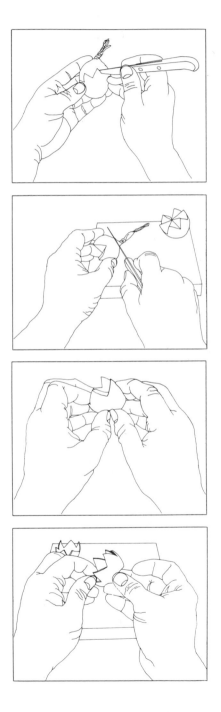

Choose an onion that is as round as possible. Avoid oval shapes or other variations in roundness. Slightly irregular onions often have double-bulb interiors, which can interfere with the cutting. You can use any size or variety of onion—Spanish, white, pearl, Bermuda, even shallots. Brush aside loose peels, but you do not have to peel the onion completely until you halve the onion.

Hold the onion in one hand, stem upward, and a paring knife in the other hand, perpendicular to the onion. Insert the knife at about the middle of the perimeter of the onion, into and just past the center of the onion. To begin the zigzag pattern, turn the blade so that it is angled at about 40 degrees. Make the angles the same for each cut. A 40-degree angle for both cuts is good for a first project. Make these alternating incisions all around the onion until the last cut intersects with the beginning of the first one. Be sure to keep the knife pointed toward the center, and hold it perpendicular to the onion for each incision. If the last angle ends up being a bit smaller than the others, that is all right.

When you have completed the zigzag, use the tips of your fingers to squeeze the onion halves and coax them apart. (A many-layered onion has a tendency to hold together tightly, even after it is cut, so you may need to go over each incision a second time.) Once the pieces are separated, remove an ample slice from the outside bottom of each half—one on the root end and one on the stem end. This cut will flatten those surfaces and expose the inner layers. Remove any remaining peel.

Grasp the outer edge of one of the onion halves with your fingers and gently nudge at the bottom with your thumbs to separate all of the layers. Reassemble all of the layers consecutively, turning each layer slightly to stagger the petals. Immerse the flower in cold water and refrigerate until you are ready to use it. An onion chrysanthemum will keep for up to three days in this state. Change the water daily.

This mock chrysanthemum can be used raw as part

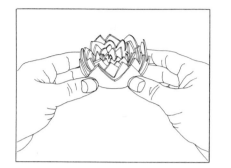

of the garnish for a platter of meat. Or you can butter a group of them, sprinkle them with salt and pepper, roast them, and serve them as a vegetable or hors d'oeuvre.

Twisted Slice

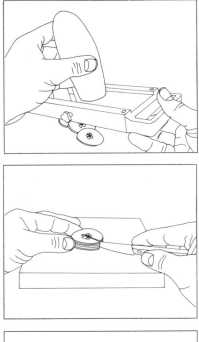

Lemons, limes, oranges, cucumbers, zucchini, and yellow squash all lend themselves well to this technique.

The secret to making the twisted slice is cutting the slices to the proper thickness. A professional cook with many years of experience can accomplish this easily, but a novice might find it an impossible task. To compensate for lack of experience, use an electric slicer, a food processor with an adjustable slicing attachment, or a *mandoline*. When using an electric slicer, you will need to trim the fruit or vegetable at both ends so that it will not roll around in the guard during slicing. *Never attempt to slice without the hand guard in place*! My thumb once required six stitches because, in my haste, I failed to use that guard. When using a food processor or a *mandoline*, keep enough pressure on the fruit or vegetable so that the slices will be uniform—$1/16$ inch or slightly thicker. They must be thin enough to be flexible when twisted, yet thick enough to stand up.

Stack six slices on a cutting board, then use a paring knife to make a partial incision all the way down from the center to the outside edge. Now take each slice, twist it, and use it as desired.

When cut, the stacked slices will keep for up to two days if wrapped air-tight in plastic wrap.

You can use a row of twisted slices on top of a salad or grilled fish, or on the side of a plate. Or create a border of them all around a platter.

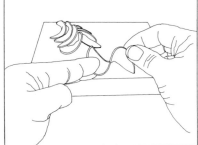

Tomato Rose

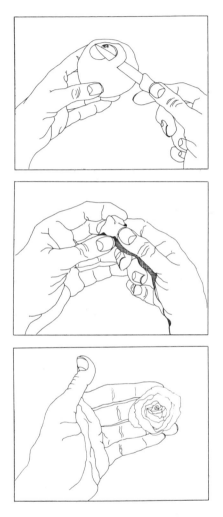

Choose a tomato with a rich, red color. It is all right if it is not perfectly round, but blemishes or breaks in the skin will interfere with the creation of the rose. Begin by using a paring knife to cut a ½- to ¾-inch-wide strip of skin, starting at the bottom of the fruit. The width of this strip can vary somewhat, as long as it is within the specified range. The strip should be roughly ¹⁄₃₂ inch thick. If it is too thin, it may break during the cutting; if it is too thick, it will be difficult to turn the strip into a rose, and the finished effort may lack finesse.

Continue cutting the strip in a spiral fashion around the fruit. Be aware of what your hands are doing; let them be relaxed. No great muscular strength is required here. Move the paring knife around the tomato in a back-and-forth sawing motion. Let the knife do the work for you. When you have a strip that is 10 to 16 inches long (depending on the width of the strip and the size of the tomato), you may end it.

Beginning at the end where you finished cutting, wrap the strip around itself. The skin should face outward, the pulp side inward. When you reach the beginning of the strip, it will wrap neatly underneath the rose, following the contour of the original tomato.

Tomato roses must be prepared on the day they will be used. They can be made in the morning if they are covered tightly with plastic wrap. Once exposed to the air, they will dry and shrivel within a few hours.

Use several tomato roses to embellish a large platter, along with a few sprigs of watercress for color. Or use a single rose to garnish a plate. I often serve poached salmon with a rose right in the center of the fillet, two celery leaves on the sides, and a vegetable cup (page 31) holding an appropriate sauce.

Tomato Blossom

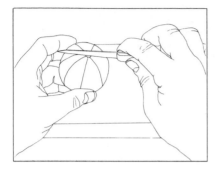

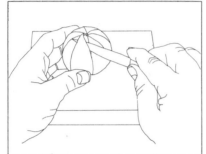

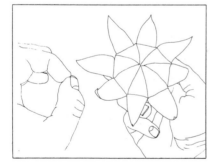

Remove the top center core of a fresh, ripe tomato by inserting a sharp paring knife outside of the core and cutting a small inverted-cone shape. Discard the core.

Invert the tomato and grasp it between the forefinger and the thumb of your free hand. With the paring knife in the other hand, create eight equidistant scores just through the skin. To do this, start at the top of one side of the tomato, then go around the bottom and up the other side. Do this three more times. These four scores will divide the tomato into eight equal parts.

Place the tomato on a cutting board and peel back the skin, one section at a time. Slip the paring knife just beneath the outer skin and separate a petal approximately three-fourths of the way down. Repeat this procedure on the remaining seven petals, then fold each petal outward.

Do not make the blossom any earlier than a half day before serving. You can score and separate the petals beforehand, scoop out the interior, and wrap the tomato tightly in plastic wrap until ready for use.

Although this piece alone makes a fine garnish, I generally scoop out the flesh and fill the cavity with watercress, some vegetable flowers, or a cold chicken salad. Reserve the scooped-out flesh for stocks, soups, or red sauces.

Leek and Scallion Brushes

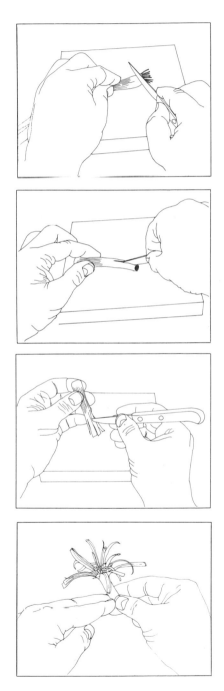

You can make leek and scallion brushes at either the root or the leaf end of these two onion varieties. Be sure that the leeks are washed well, because there usually is sand between their leaves.

With a utility knife, remove the root, then sever the leaves where they first begin to grow away from the main part of the stem. The remaining piece should be 3 or more inches long. Remove any loose or spoiled outer layers. The leek and scallion leaves that you remove are useful for flavoring stocks or soups. Finely chopped scallions are excellent in salads, and the light green inner leaves of leeks are magnificent when blanched in salted water or stock, drained, chilled, and marinated in a vinaigrette.

Use a paring knife to make a 2-inch-long cut directly down the center of the onion. This will partially split the scallion or leek from one end of the segment. Roll the partially split segment 90 degrees. This will position the first cut horizontally (or parallel to the horizontal plane of the cutting board). Holding the two split ends together with the forefinger and thumb of your free hand, make another 2-inch-long cut directly down the center. This will produce four equally split 2-inch-long quarters, still connected at the left end. Lift this piece with the fingers of your free hand, and, using the tip of the knife, shred each of the quarters into two or more strips. Each of these strips should be the same length as the first two cuts. A leek brush requires more "shreds" because it is so much larger. Whereas a scallion might need two or three "shreds" per quarter, a leek will require anywhere from five to twelve per quarter.

The brush "petals" will curl outward if you place the leek or scallion in cold water. The longer they are in water, the more the brushes will curl. A brush will keep for up to two days if immersed in cold water and refrigerated, but it is best to use it after one day.

Scallion brushes are traditionally part of Peking Duck but can be used in any dish in which the taste of raw onion is appropriate—salads, pâtés, steak tartar, any roast.

Cucumber Fan and Loops

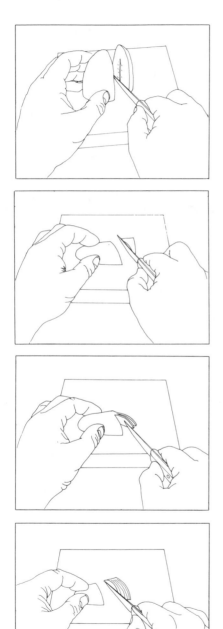

Wash a firm, fresh, large salad cucumber in tepid water with some natural soap. (Cucumbers are often coated with oil or wax to preserve them. To remove this coating, use Ivory soap, Dr. Bronner's peppermint soap, or some other natural soap.)

Using a paring knife, cut a 3-inch-long segment off one end. Place this little dome so that the cut surface rests on a cutting board. Make a vertical cut to remove roughly one-fourth of the segment, slicing all the way down to the board. (By cutting only one-fourth of the way into the cucumber, you can avoid having large center seeds in the severed piece.) Now tip over the small piece so that the newly cut side is flat on the board. (The piece should be lying horizontally in front of you.) From the cut end, remove a small triangular piece, at roughly a 20-degree angle, and discard it. Taking the larger piece, make an uneven number (five, seven, or nine) of incomplete slices, 1/32 to 1/64 inch apart, exactly parallel, cutting through to the board. The "petals" of the fan must be cut thin enough to bend without breaking, and *must* be perfectly parallel. Your paring knife must be razor-sharp, because this garnish cannot be made with a dull knife. Be sure that all of the slices remain connected at the top.

At the fifth, seventh, or ninth slice (depending on which number you have made), sever the section from the rest of the cucumber piece. Firmly press the small cut piece down and to one side from the top center, so the slices fan out.

You can also make cucumber loops out of the fan. Simply fold over every other "petal," beginning with the second one from either outside edge. The angles created by all of the previous cuts, plus the pressure at the base of each two "petals," will keep the loops in place.

These garnishes will stay fresh for most of one day if you place them on a small plate, wrap them tightly with plastic wrap, and refrigerate them.

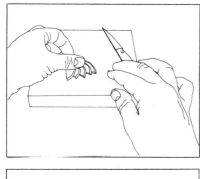

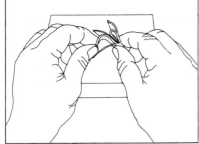

Spiky Leek Leaves

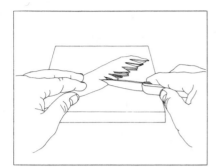

This garnish is similar to the cut-paper snowflakes we made in grade-school art classes. Remember taking a small square of paper, folding it into eighths, rounding the corners, and snipping small triangles from the edges to create a snowflake? Leek leaves are naturally doubled over, and any pattern cut into a leaf will be repeated when the leaf is opened up.

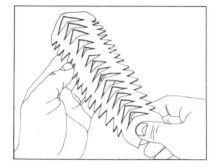

Put a folded leaf down on a cutting board, then use a paring knife to cut a series of V or triangle shapes along both edges. You can make these little triangles any width, any length, any angle. Experiment with various angles to create different patterns. When you have completed several leaves, cut them to different lengths for variety.

These garnishes can be prepared up to two days in advance. Immerse them in cold water and refrigerate. Change the water daily. The longer the leaves remain in the water, the more the spikes will curl.

Use spiky leek leaves as part of a small grouping of vegetable flowers.

Vegetable Cups

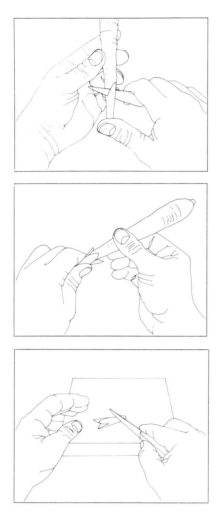

If Ludwig Mies van der Rohe had been speaking of food rather than architecture when he said, "Less is more," he probably would have been referring to this garnish—simple and unpretentious, yet magnificent in its simplicity. You can make cups from carrots, cucumbers, zucchini, and yellow squash.

If you are using a carrot, peel it first. At the tapered root end, use a paring knife to make three angled cuts from the outside edge of the carrot, starting roughly 1½ inches up from the tapered end. Cut down and in, and cut no farther than one-fourth of the width of the carrot. The angle should be roughly 55 degrees. Cut three elliptically shaped petals. The base juncture of each petal should intersect with the base juncture of the petal next to it. When you have cut the three petals, the cup will still be attached to the rest of the carrot; to remove it, twist the cup away from the rest of the carrot. Cut a small piece from the bottom of the cup to allow it to stand.

You can make additional cups all the way up the carrot, cucumber, or squash.

Carrot cups will last up to four days if immersed in cold water and refrigerated. Change the water daily. Stored in the same manner, cucumber cups will keep for two days, squash cups for three days.

Small vegetable cups, such as those made from carrots or baby zucchini, can be used as one element of a small garnish grouping. Larger cups, made from cucumbers or larger squash, can be scooped out with a Parisienne scoop, sliced along the bottom so they will stand, and then used as containers for hot or cold sauce. You might use them, for example, for hollandaise sauce with poached salmon, herb mayonnaise with crudités, or chutney sauce with prawns in beer batter.

Double-Petaled Carrot Cups

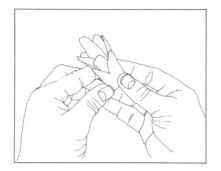

These are a variation on vegetable cups (page 31) and sculptured roses (page 56).

Choose a moderately fat carrot and peel it. At the tapered root end, use a paring knife to make three angled cuts from the outside edge of the carrot, starting roughly 1½ inches up from the tapered end. Cut down and in at a sharp angle, roughly 55 degrees. Cut three elliptically shaped petals. The base juncture of each petal should intersect with the base juncture of the petal next to it.

Before cutting the second row of petals, remove a small slice of carrot from behind each of the petals in the first row. This creates a small space behind each petal. Cut a second row of petals in the same fashion as the first row, each second petal directly inside the first. The second row should be cut deep enough so that the double-flower cup can be twisted and snapped away from the rest of the carrot. Cut a small piece from the bottom of the flower to allow it to stand.

If you prefer, you can stagger the second row of petals. Each petal in the second row is then exactly between the two just in front of it. The technique for this is the same. Remove a thin slice of carrot at the juncture just above and directly between two petals from the row in front. Then cut the second row of petals above and behind that point, twist, and remove the cup.

These cups will keep for up to four days if immersed in cold water and refrigerated. Change the water daily.

As with vegetable cups, double-petaled carrot cups can be used to hold any hot or cold sauce to accompany an hors d'oeuvre or a main course.

California *mukimono*

Zucchini Crown

Onion Chrysanthemum
and Twisted Slices

Tomato Rose and Cucumber
Fan and Loops

Scallion Brush and Vegetable
Cups made from carrots

Imprinted Mushrooms with Radish Chrysanthemums and Mushrooms

Turnip Sunflower and Carrot Spider Chrysanthemums

Onion Artichoke and Carrot Pansy

Sculptured Roses made from rutabaga, purpletop turnip, and beet

Calla Lily

Lattice Squash Collar and Cucumber Timbale

Cucumber Boat and two variations of
the Looped Lemon

Celery Sea Anemone
and Cabbage Blossom

Apple Dove, Apple and Pear Feathers, and Rococo Apple

Staircase and Sushi Garnish

New York Food Show, 1985; "Edible Centerpiece." *Photograph by Steve Brigidi.*

"Eat Your Art Out," Museum of University of California, Berkeley, food sculpture show, 1981. *Photograph by D. P. Larousse.*

Mushroom Imprints

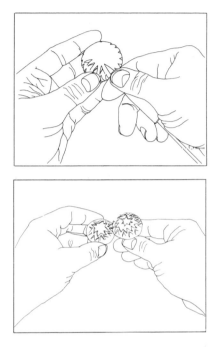

Mushroom imprints might be called "the poor man's fluted mushroom." Fluted, or turned, mushrooms involve a classic technique that can take years to master. Fluting a mushroom requires a simultaneous cutting-and-scraping cut, which leaves a series of curved ridges running from the top center out to the bottom edges. Not until two years after graduating from culinary school did I develop any real proficiency with that technique.

Imprinting is a much simpler process. Holding the blade of a fine-pointed paring knife between your thumb and forefinger roughly ½ inch from the knife tip, press the tip ⅛ inch into the flesh of a large, fresh, white mushroom cap held in the other hand.

There are no other specific rules governing this garnish. You can create any design you wish by varying the shape of the knife point, the direction of the knife, and the complexity of the pattern. There is considerable room for creativity. I make new pattern variations every time I pick up a mushroom.

Imprinted mushrooms should be brushed immediately with fresh lemon juice so they will not turn brown. (Never wash mushrooms by immersing them in water for any length of time because they are both delicate and porous. Wipe them clean with a clean towel or with a pastry brush dipped in lemon juice. The latter combines washing and color protection in one step.) Serve the mushroom imprints soon after preparing them; even when brushed with lemon juice, the mushrooms stay fresh for only a few hours.

An imprinted raw mushroom is a distinctive garnish for a salad. If poached in white wine, butter, and a few drops of lemon juice, it can embellish a mushroom omelette, grilled meat or poultry, or any other dish that calls for mushrooms.

Radish Chrysanthemum and Mushroom

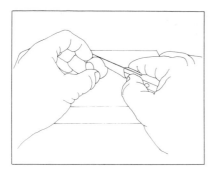

Radishes lend themselves well to sculpting for several reasons. First, the bright red exterior contrasts well with the white interior; second, radishes keep well if immersed in cold water; and third, their crisp texture responds well to a sharp paring knife.

To make a radish chrysanthemum, first use a paring knife to flatten the radish at both root and stem ends. One of these cuts should be just enough to keep the tuber from rolling, while the second cut should extend about one-third of the way into the radish to expose a fairly large part of the interior. Make a series of parallel vertical slices, approximately ¹⁄₁₆ inch apart, from one side of the radish to the other. Make these incisions only in one direction, to ensure straight lines. The depth of each of these cuts should be roughly ¼ inch shy of the bottom of the radish, although each cut will vary in depth, depending on the contour of the radish.

Repeat this procedure, making parallel cuts perpendicular to the first set of parallel cuts, thus creating a grid pattern. The depth of these second cuts should also be roughly ¼ inch shy of the bottom.

Immerse the radish in cold water and refrigerate. Overnight, the radish will open up to resemble a miniature chrysanthemum.

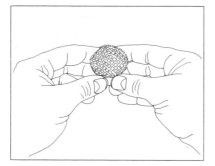

When choosing radishes for making mushrooms, look for a fresh bunch with tops still attached—this usually means there will be a fine root strand. Even though the garnish can be made either with or without this root, it adds a unique touch to what will become the top of a baby radish mushroom.

With a paring knife, cut away the green top of a radish, along with roughly one-fifth of the radish. Turn the vegetable so that this just-cut side faces downward and the root points upward. Score the radish all the way around, one-third of the way down from the root. This score should be parallel to the flat surface and approximately ¼ inch deep. Next invert the radish so the root points downward. Make a series of cuts, angled inward, to create the stem of the

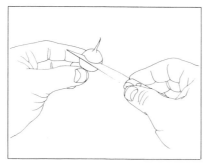

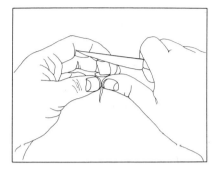

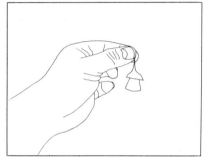

mushroom, fat at its base and thinner toward the underside of the cap. Each mushroom will take on a slightly different shape, depending on its original configuration.

Both mums and mushrooms will keep well for up to four days if immersed in cold water and refrigerated. Change the water daily.

Use mums and mushrooms as salad or entrée garnishes.

Radish Fan and Feather

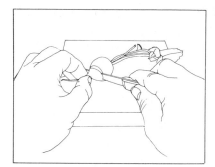

The radish fan is a variation on the radish chrysanthemum (page **34**). In some vegetable markets and at certain times of the year, you can purchase radishes with their green leaves still attached. Making a fan from a leafy radish is a colorful way to serve this vegetable as part of a tray of crudités. If there are no leaves, trim a small slice from each end of a radish. Otherwise, trim a slice only from the root end. With a paring knife, make a series of parallel cuts into the radish approximately ⅛ inch apart. Cut to within ¼ inch of the leafy end, keeping the slices connected there.

Immerse the radish in cold water and refrigerate. Overnight, the slices will fan out.

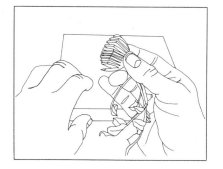

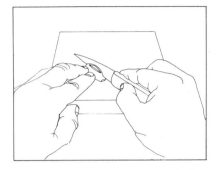

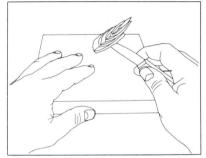

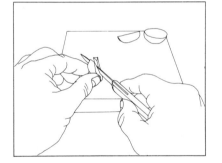

The radish feather is a variation on the apple dove and rococo apple (page **82**).

With a paring knife, trim the two ends of a radish to flatten them slightly. Split the radish lengthwise into four equal quarters. Hold each wedge vertically and flatten the sharp edge by slicing off a thin strip. Each wedge should now lie flat on a cutting board with the curved side of each piece facing up.

Beginning at the center top of the curved part of a radish quarter, cut a **V**-shaped piece, a small, 45-degree-angled wedge. Next, make parallel cuts on both sides of the first wedge to create a series of wedges, one on top of the other. Because radishes are small, you will be able to cut only three to five wedges into the radish. Be sure that each wedge is cut completely so that it can be separated from the radish.

The cut wedges can be left in place in the radish and covered tightly with plastic wrap. They should be used the same day they are made. Just before serving, slide the wedges out of the radish toward one end to create the feather effect.

Use radish fans and feathers in groupings of flowers or as garnishes for canapés.

The same technique can be used for apples, citrus fruit, and melons.

Carrot Stars

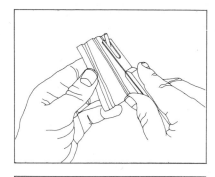

With a utility knife, trim the ends of a large carrot, peel it, and cut a 3-inch-long segment. Hold the segment in one hand and a channel knife in the other. Cut a series of lengthwise grooves all around the perimeter of the piece. Depending on the thickness of the carrot and the design you want to create, you might cut six or eight grooves.

Place the segment horizontally on a cutting board. Using a French knife, cut the segment into slices $\frac{1}{16}$ inch thick to create star shapes. For a variation on the straight perpendicular slices, try cutting the stars slightly on the bias.

Carrot stars will keep for up to four days if immersed in cold water and refrigerated. Change the water daily.

Use a single star or a stack of five or six of them, fanned out. If you like, sauté stars in butter and fresh herbs and serve them as the vegetable *du jour*.

Carrot Cones

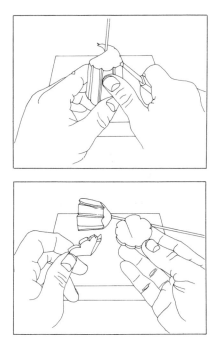

This is an expanded version of carrot stars (page 38).

With a utility knife, trim the ends of a large carrot, peel it, and cut a 3-inch-long segment. Hold the segment in one hand and a channel knife in the other. Cut a series of lengthwise grooves all around the perimeter of the piece. Depending on the thickness of the carrot and design you want to create, you might cut six or eight grooves.

Insert a bamboo skewer or toothpick into the center of one end of the carrot segment. (The toothpick or skewer should be parallel to the length of the carrot.) Holding a paring knife in one hand and the carrot in the other (skewer or toothpick pointing up), set the cutting edge of the blade lightly against the toothpick, close to where it enters the carrot. Tip the paring-knife handle downward and begin rotating the carrot into the knife blade. The knife should continue to be positioned against the skewer guide. As you cut into the carrot, continue to work the knife downward, forming the inverted conical shape that will become the outside of the first cone. The angle of this conical shape should be about 45 degrees.

When you complete this inverted cone shape and clear away the trimmed carrot, begin cutting the carrot cone. Keeping the paring knife blade set lightly against the skewer at a 45-degree angle, cut carefully around the cone shape and remove a cone-shaped carrot segment $1/16$ inch thick. When you have worked the knife around one complete turn plus an additional $1/8$ inch, sever the piece from the rest of the carrot. Now carefully lift the cone up off the skewer. (As you continue to cut carrot cones from the carrot segment, the skewer guide will become slightly loose. Push the skewer further into the center as you work.)

Carrot cones will keep for up to four days if immersed in cold water and refrigerated. Change the water daily.

This is an especially versatile and eye-pleasing flower garnish. It can be used as a canapé base or stuffed with a seasoned cream cheese and a black olive.

Chili-Pepper Flower

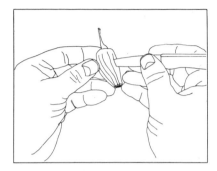

Choose a long, unblemished green or red chili pepper or jalapeño. (It is a good idea to wear close-fitting rubber gloves when working with hot chilies. The oils can burn your skin.)

Use a paring knife to remove a ½-inch slice from the tapered end of the chili. Holding the blade of a paring knife between your thumb and forefinger, make a series of lengthwise incisions in the pepper. Each cut should begin about ¼ inch from the stem end and extend down through the snipped-off end. Make each cut just a little deeper than the shell of the pepper, but be careful not to disturb the center part of the chili, where all the seeds are. (The seeds will become the center, or pistil, of the flower.)

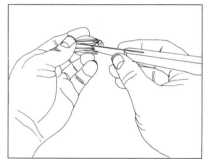

Insert the knife carefully at the snipped end and make sure that each strip is disconnected from the seeds.

Immerse the pepper in cold water overnight, allowing the strips to curl outward.

This garnish will keep for up to two additional days if immersed in cold water and refrigerated. Change the water daily.

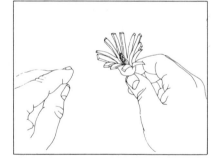

Chili-pepper flowers are very colorful in a small grouping of flowers.

Garlic Bud

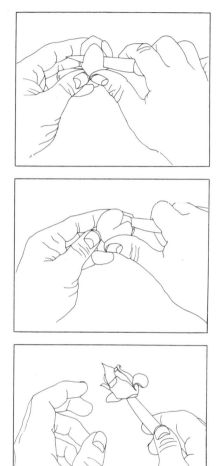

This project employs a technique similar to that used for vegetable cups (page **31**) and double-petaled carrot cups (page **32**). The primary difference is one of scale.

Choose a large garlic clove that is as rounded as you can find and peel it. Elephant garlic is a good choice for this flower, as its cloves are so large. Holding the top of the clove so it points upward, use a paring knife to make three to five angled cuts from the outside edge of the clove, starting roughly halfway down the clove. Cut down and in, and cut no farther than one-third of the width of the clove. The angle should be 55 to 60 degrees. Because of the curve of the clove, the petals will be elliptically shaped. The base juncture of each petal should intersect with the base juncture of the petal next to it.

Cut a second row of petals in the same fashion, locating it above and behind the first row.

Immerse the clove in cold water and refrigerate. Overnight, the petals will curl outward.

Garlic buds will keep for up to three additional days if immersed in cold water and refrigerated. Change the water daily.

Serve as a raw garnish to garlic aficionados with any dish that contains an abundance of garlic.

Part II | **MORE COMPLEX FORMS**

White-Turnip Calla Lily

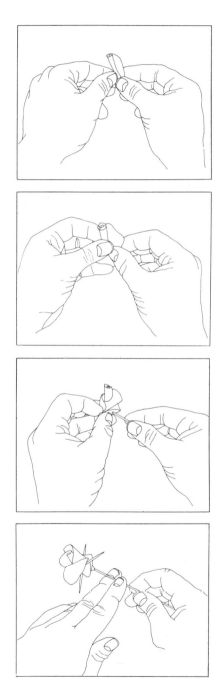

This flower requires the use of an electric slicer or a *mandoline*. The turnip can be just about any size, depending on what size you wish the flower to be. (A good size to begin with is 2½- to 3-inch-wide slices.) You will need three or four slices, each slightly less than ¹⁄₁₆ inch thick. The thickness of these slices is critical. They have to be rolled to make the flower, and if they are too thick, they will snap when rolled.

There is no need to peel the turnip. The various shades of lavender on its top half add interesting lines of color to the finished flower.

Start the flower by taking one of the slices and rolling it up like a cigarette. When rolled, it should be ³⁄₈ inch wide. To keep it from unrolling, hold it gently between your forefinger and thumb.

Take a second slice and wrap it around the first roll. Again, hold it all in place gently between your forefinger and thumb. Peel back the top portion of the second slice, just enough so that it stays in that folded-back position. Take a third slice and insert it into the space between the end of the second slice and the rest of the flower. (Insert it just enough so that when it is wrapped around, it will look like a petal of the flower.) Wrap this third slice around, then peel back the top portion. Position the third slice so that when folded back, it is opposite the foldback of the second slice. (Once you become familiar with this technique, you can work more slices into the piece. Try using four or five slices.) Insert two toothpicks, crossing each other through the center, to secure the calla lily.

The lily will keep well for up to a week if immersed immediately in cold water and refrigerated. Change the water daily.

Use small calla lilies as an individual plate garnish and larger ones for platters.

Turnip Sunflower

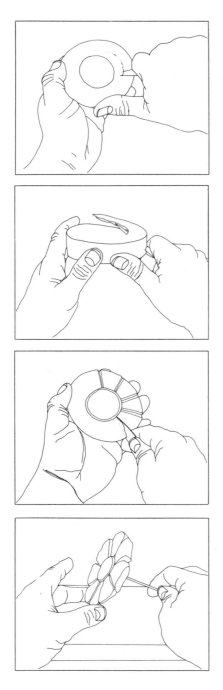

With a utility knife, remove a slice approximately 1 inch thick from one end of a turnip or a rutabaga (another name for a Swedish turnip). Parallel to that plane, cut another slice 1¼ to 1½ inches thick. Due to the contour of the turnip, one side of this thicker slice will be a slightly smaller circle than the other side. Holding the slice so the smaller circle faces upward, use a paring knife to work on the inside edge. Carve away enough of the turnip to make a 45-degree angle all around the circumference, starting at ¼ inch up from the wide-side edge and going toward the center of the smaller side. Trim any peel from the remaining ¼-inch-thick side portion.

Now turn the slice so that the larger circle faces upward. With the tip of the paring knife, score a circle in the center of the slice. This circle should be no greater in diameter than one-half of the diameter of the slice. Make the score about ¼ inch deep. Just outside this score, pare away, at roughly a 20-degree angle, enough of the turnip to extend down to the base of the ¼-inch-thick section. This will leave a flat-topped pillbox form in the center. Soften the outside edge of this pillbox by paring away its sharp corners.

If you are faced with preparing a large quantity of these flowers, a set of concentric circle cutters can save time. I use a large one occasionally to cut out the outer contour of the flower, and then I use a smaller cutter to make the center score.

Cut a series of shallow V-shaped grooves from the outside perimeter of the center section to the outside of the entire slice. Each groove should emanate from the center of the flower, and the distance between the grooves should be ¾ to 1 inch. Cut grooves all the way around the slice. They will outline the petals of the sunflower.

To define these petals a bit more, cut a V-shaped groove, this time perpendicular to the face of the flower, in the center of each of the previously cut grooves. With the paring knife, smooth the sharp corners created by these second grooves.

This garnish will keep well for up to two weeks if

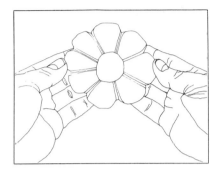

immersed in cold water and refrigerated. Change the water daily.

For turnip lovers, blanch a number of these flowers in lightly salted boiling water until nearly tender. Brush them with butter, sprinkle with brown sugar and a pinch of nutmeg, and bake until nicely glazed.

Variations in the shape and position of the center circle, and in the sizes of the petals, are always possible with a sculptured piece such as this sunflower. As the cook, you are the sculptor here, and these variations reveal your particular style.

Spider Chrysanthemum

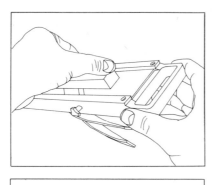

For this project, you will need to use an electric slicer or a Japanese *mandoline*. Choose a fat carrot with as little taper as possible.

With a paring knife, slice off the top end of the carrot, then cut a 6-inch-long segment. Shape this 6-inch-long segment, using the utility knife, into a rectangle 6 inches long and 1 inch wide. Now slice this segment on the slicer, or *mandoline*, into $\frac{1}{16}$-inch-thick slices. Reject any slices that are not uniform—they should be 6 x 1 x $\frac{1}{16}$ inches. Stack them in pairs on the cutting board.

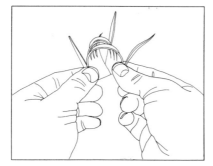

On one of the pairs of slices, insert the point of the paring knife into the carrot $\frac{3}{4}$ inch in from one end and $\frac{1}{8}$ inch in from the side. From there, cut down the length of the carrot, toward you, angling the knife slightly toward the outside edge. After cutting $2\frac{1}{2}$ to 3 inches down the slices, your knife will reach the edge of the slices. This will leave a sharply pointed strip, $2\frac{1}{2}$ to 3 inches long, that is still attached at a point $\frac{3}{4}$ inch from one end. Turn the slices around and repeat this procedure on the same side, beginning at the opposite end. Make the incision exactly the same as the first one. The two strips will overlap. Repeat these two cuts on the opposite side of the two stacked slices.

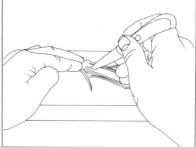

In the remaining center area, make two, three, or four parallel incisions down the center. These incisions should begin and end where the spiky pieces do, about $\frac{3}{4}$ inch from each end. Be sure that these center incisions do not sever any part of the carrot.

Carefully lift one of the two slices, avoiding breaking off any of the fragile parts, and grasp one end between the thumb and forefinger of each hand. Now turn each end in a semicircular direction so that a corner of one end rests flat on a corner of the other end. At this point, the corners of these two ends will not be lined up perfectly.

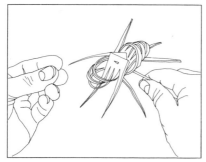

Spear these ends with a toothpick. Repeat the twist/turn movement with the other slice, turn it to face the first slice, and push the second slice onto the same toothpick.

Cut two $\frac{1}{4}$-inch-thick round slices from the original carrot and push them onto the toothpick from both sides, to secure the mum. Any excess toothpick extending from the slice of carrot inside the flower can either be capped with a black olive or cherry tomato or trimmed so that it will not show.

Immerse the flower in cold water and refrigerate. Overnight, the eight finely slivered pieces will fan out in different directions and curl in unpredictable ways. The cold water crisps them and holds them in place. They will keep this way for up to four days. Change the water daily.

A carrot mum can be used as a garnish for a salad or any variety of cold platter in which the color and texture of a crisp carrot would be appropriate.

Chili-Pepper Bud

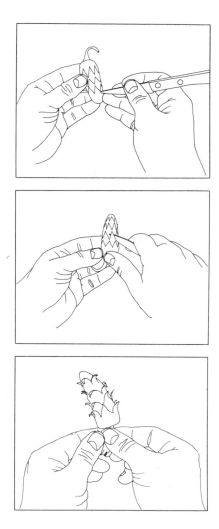

For this magnificent little garnish, choose a fresh, smooth, unblemished 2- to 3-inch-long hot pepper, the type marketed either as chilies or jalapeños. They come in a variety of colors and intensities: light green, dark green, and bright red. Ask a grocer to show you the milder ones. Choose one of these, because a full-strength chili or jalapeño can be too powerful to those unaccustomed to this spicy fare. (It is a good idea to wear close-fitting rubber gloves when working with hot chilies. The oils can burn your skin.)

Holding the pepper stem in your free hand, grasp the tip of a *very* sharp paring knife with your cutting hand. Hold the knife much as you would a pencil, about ½ inch from the point. Starting near the stem, cut a series of zigzags at 20- or 25-degree angles, just barely scoring the skin of the chili. This skin is rather thin, and it is the only part of the pepper that requires scoring for this garnish. Be particularly careful in doing this, because the underlying flesh of the pepper, also thin, does not allow much leeway for overscoring. If you cut through the fleshy part of the pepper, you will weaken the structure of the whole piece. The zigzag cuts should be roughly ⅜ inch high. Complete the zigzag around the pepper, with the last score ending at the beginning of the first one.

Score a second row of zigzags around the outside, just below the first row. The only difference here is that you stagger the petals this time. Each zigzag point in the second row should be centered between the two points above it. Continue until you have done four or five rows of zigzags.

Starting with the row of zigzags farthest from the stem, peel away part of the skin from the chili. Use the tip of the paring knife, tucking it under the skin and slicing into the area between the skin and the underlying flesh, so that *only* the paper-thin skin is separated from the rest of the pepper. (The parts that you peel away are the triangular shapes that point downward from the stem.) When the skin is peeled away, it should remain attached at its base (the bottom of each triangle). Repeat this all the way down the chili pepper.

This can be a frustrating project to tackle, since the spacing is all rather minute and there is little room for error, but be patient—it is worth the effort.

Immerse the pepper in cold water and refrigerate. After a half day, the peeled skin will curl away from the rest of the pepper. This will keep for up to three days if immersed in cold water and refrigerated. Change the water daily.

Use the chili-pepper bud as a special platter garnish.

Carrot Pansy

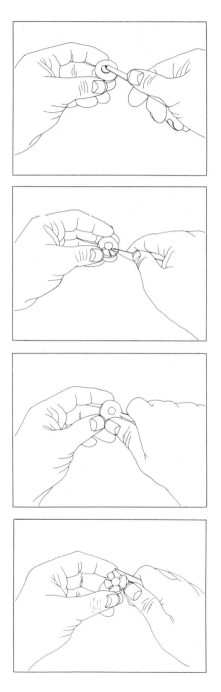

This flower is a smaller-scale version of the turnip sunflower (page **46**).

Choose a fat carrot and peel it. With a paring knife, cut off the broader end, then slice a ½-inch-thick segment from this end of the carrot. Score a small circle ¼ inch in diameter in the center of one side of this slice, using a miniature Parisienne, or *pois*, scoop. If you do not have a *pois* scoop, the circle can be scored with the tip of a paring knife, although the miniature scoop scores a cleaner circle than a paring knife can.

Using the tip of a paring knife, pare away a portion of the slice just outside this center circle, leaving a pillbox shape in the center. Lightly trim the top outside edges of the pillbox to make the edges less sharp.

On the top surface of the carrot slice, make five grooves, each one extending from the outside edge of the pillbox to the edge of the flower. These grooves should be equidistant from one another, but slightly uneven proportions are not a cause for concern. Once you have cut these grooves, you will have outlined the five petals of the flower.

Soften all of the outside edges by paring them down slightly until they are rounded. Also trim the lower outside edges of the flower, so that the petals are thinner on the outside edges than they are at the center.

An interesting variation of this technique is using the five-sided Chinese vegetable flower cutters discussed in the *Tools* section (page **16**). Using the cutters, punch out any flower shape from the ½-inch carrot slices. Proceed as explained above; instead of having to shape the circular piece by hand, the pansy will be pentagonal, or five-sided.

Carrot pansies will keep for up to four days if immersed in cold water and refrigerated. Change the water daily.

An ambitious cook might blanch these flowers in lightly salted boiling water, drain them, toss them in butter, and serve them as a vegetable. A single pansy makes an attractive component in a small garnish grouping if impaled on a toothpick. (Add a scallion leaf to sheathe the toothpick.)

Onion Artichoke

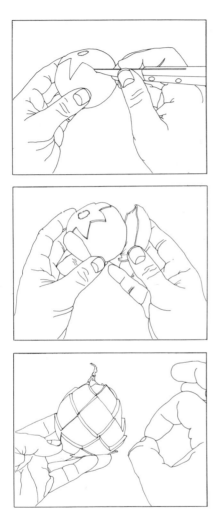

Choose a large Spanish, white, or Bermuda onion. Because much of the onion is removed in the process of making this garnish, it is wise to begin with a fairly large specimen of whatever variety you choose.

With a paring knife, remove a very thin slice of onion from the bottom, or core end, of the onion. (Only a very thin slice is cut from this end, to ensure that the onion will remain intact and the garnish will hold together.) If a brown stem extends from the other side of the onion, leave it. It can be trimmed after the flower is completed, or you may allow a portion of it to remain, as part of the finished flower.

Remove the outer skin, then turn the onion upside down so that the stem end (where the core holds it together) faces you. Holding a paring knife between your thumb and forefinger, score a zigzag around the top side not quite 1 inch down from the top. The zigzag cuts should be ½ inch in length. Be careful when scoring; each incision should be only as deep as the outside layer of the onion. (Onion layers are roughly $\frac{1}{16}$ to $\frac{1}{8}$ inch thick.) Because there is no way to determine exactly how deep the knife point is extending through the outside layer, you must estimate the thickness of each layer and make the incisions accordingly. This becomes easier with practice. It is better to make the incisions a little too shallow rather than too deep. If they are too shallow, you can always rescore them to the proper depth. If they are too deep, some of the petals may fall off later. By experimenting with different lengths and widths of zigzags, you can achieve myriad different results with this technique.

Once you have completed the first round of zigzag incisions, make another score just through that first layer. Run it downward from any one of the arrow points to the bottom of the bulb. Set the knife down. With your fingertips, reach into this last incision and pull away the entire outside layer of onion. The row of arrow shapes from the first layer should be left on top of the now-exposed second layer of onion. (Save the removed onion layers for seasoning or for onion soup.)

Run a second round of zigzag incisions directly below the first one, again cutting only one layer deep. Stagger the incisions so that the point of each arrow shape falls between two points of the previous round. When you have completed the second round, make a vertical incision in that layer only. The incision should run downward from any one of the arrow points in the second layer. Remove the excess part of the second layer just as you did with the first one. This will leave a second round of petals, staggered in relation to the first round. Continue this procedure until you have covered the entire onion with rows of elevated arrow-shaped petals, leaving a mock artichoke.

This garnish will keep for up to a week if immersed in cold water and refrigerated. Change the water daily.

Use onion artichokes as platter garnishes or roast them with herbs and butter or olive oil and serve them as appetizers or vegetables.

As you develop skill with the cutting technique shown here, try working with smaller onions, such as pearls, small whites, even shallots.

Sculptured Rose

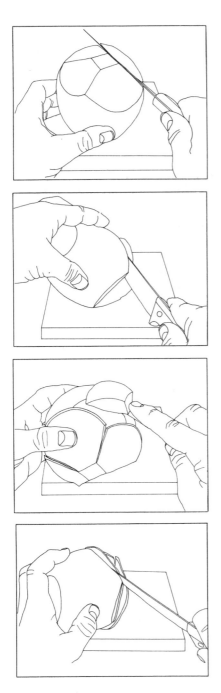

With all garnishing techniques, each cook and chef develops an individual style. Sculptured roses seem to reveal more than most about a particular chef's individuality.

Carved roses have always been difficult for me. To fashion them well, you need to develop great dexterity with a knife. Discouraged with trying to do them well during my early training, I never spent much time on the technique and worked more on the rest of my repertoire.

More recently, however, another teacher was gracious enough to show me his technique for carving roses. It is very simple, and the resulting flowers are the finest I have ever seen. He works with a variety of root vegetables—beets, white turnips, and rutabaga. Rutabaga seems to me to be the best choice for learning this skill because its large size allows you to see what you are doing. Also, its texture is firm, yet pliable enough to respond to a knife blade. White turnips are perhaps too small in diameter, and beets, also small, leave red dye all over your hands and work area, which can be discouraging.

To begin, take a paring knife and peel a small- to medium-sized yellow turnip, or rutabaga. Peel away only a thin layer, and try to avoid creating ridges and uneven areas. With a French knife, remove a 1- to 1½-inch-thick slice from the bottom of the turnip.

Tip the turnip so that its flattened bottom surface faces you. Lightly score a ¾-inch square in the center of the bottom. Placing the blade of the fillet knife along one of the scored sides of the square, cut down and out at a 45-degree angle. Slice off and discard this piece. Cut off three more pieces in the same manner. The remaining square section will become the bottom of the rose, while the four just-exposed surfaces will be the outside surfaces of the first row of four petals.

To make the petals, set the turnip down on one of the four angled surfaces. Fashion the first petal by slicing into the turnip parallel to the angled surface facing you. This incision should begin at exactly the point where the cut surface meets the outside of the

turnip. The beginning part of the petal should be paper-thin, but as you move the knife down and toward the center of the turnip, petal thickness should increase to a maximum of ⅛ inch. (Each petal must be paper-thin at the top edge so that it will later curl in water. The thinner the petal at this outside edge, the more delicate the rose. The petals should be thicker inside to give the flower stability.) Be careful not to cut too far into the center of the turnip. With several rows of petals still to be cut, there is always a danger of cutting too far and weakening the structure of the rose. This all takes considerable dexterity. Practice will improve your technique.

Once you have completed the first round of four petals, begin the second round. First, you need to cut away four more pieces. This second round of cutaways is staggered—each one is located directly behind the junction of two petals of the first row. When this second set of cutaways has been removed, leaving four new flat surfaces, repeat the petal-cutting technique, exactly as you did on the first round. Fashion successive rounds of petals in exactly the same way—cut away four staggered pieces, then make four petals in those locations. Continue until you reach the top of the rose. As you reach the last round or two of petals, you may be working in a very confined cutting space. To compensate for this, decrease the number of petals in each round from four to three.

Immerse the turnip in cold water and refrigerate. After the first day, the petals will curl and curve, giving the rose its delicate finished appearance.

Turnip and beet roses keep well for up to three weeks if immersed in cold water and refrigerated. Change the water daily. (Store beet roses separately, however, to prevent their strong color from dyeing turnip roses.)

A half-dozen beet and turnip roses add a stunning element to a platter of roasted meats, poultry, or game.

Sushi Garnish

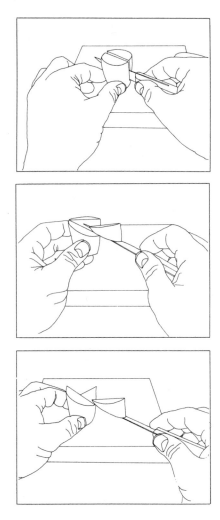

To my knowledge, there is no official Japanese word for this garnish, but it is often used with sushi and sashimi. I have seen it made with zucchini, cucumber, a piece of cooked egg, and even a molded piece of tofu. For this exercise, I will explain how to fashion it from a cucumber.

With a paring knife, slice off the end of an unpeeled cucumber, then cut a 2- to 2½-inch-long segment. Stand this segment upright on a cutting board. (If the piece varies in width, the wider part of the segment should be at the top.) At exactly the center of the top of the segment, cut downward, perpendicular to the board, roughly halfway. Hold the segment in your free hand and make a 45-degree-angled cut from the outside toward this partial split to sever a small wedge. The incision should run from the lowest point of the perpendicular cut to the top point of the same cut. Repeat the wedge removal, in reverse, on the other half of the segment. Two opposing sloping planes should remain, creating a sort of optical illusion.

This garnish will keep for two days if immersed in cold water and refrigerated. Change the water daily.

To add another dimension to this piece, you can cut three or four feathers on the outside of the sushi garnish, just below the slope. The technique for this is similar to that used for the apple dove and rococo apple (page **82**).

Turn the sushi garnish on its side and place it on a cutting board with one of the sloped planes clearly in view. Cut a small **V**-shaped wedge at a 55-degree angle into the side of the cucumber, parallel to the sloped plane, and about ⅛ inch deep. There should be approximately a ½-inch space between this wedge and the sloped edge that runs parallel to it. Cut a second **V** about ⅛ inch deeper, wider, and longer than the first **V**. Cut a third wedge that is slightly larger than the second. Cut a fourth if space will allow. At this point, the severed wedges should be assembled in their original position. Cut a set of wedges on the opposite side, in exactly the same manner.

With the tip of a paring knife, gently slide the first wedge outward and upward, ⅛ to ¼ inch. Repeat with the set on the opposite side.

The addition of the feathers shortens the life of this garnish, so prepare this on the same day that it will be served. The wedges can remain in their original position, and the piece can be wrapped in plastic wrap and refrigerated until ready for use.

Inverted Eight-Petaled Flower

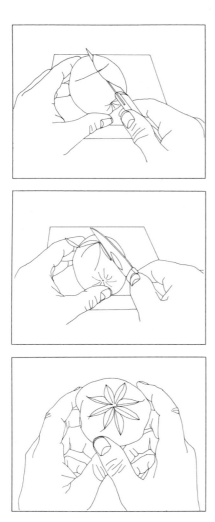

This Asian flower motif may seem a bit abstract at first, because it is inverted, or made in reverse.

An apple is a good fruit for this project. Stand it, unpeeled, upright on a cutting board. With a utility knife, remove a ½-inch-thick slice from one side of the apple. Place the cut surface flat on the board. Position the cutting edge of a paring knife on the center of the apple, parallel to the core. Tip the paring knife to the right, at a 45-degree angle, and slice a 2-inch-long incision (approximately) into the apple to a depth of ¼ inch or so. Return the knife to the original intersection point and tip the knife to the left at a 45-degree angle. Slice inward another ¼ inch or so. What remains is an inverted V shape with its point on the surface. (Although the knife blade is flat and straight, each of these ¼-inch-deep cuts is curved because of the shape of the apple.) At this point, nothing has been removed from the apple. (The tiny wedges created by the series of cuts will not come out until after the third and fourth sets of cuts.)

Now repeat the first two incisions, but make them exactly perpendicular to the first set so that they cross in the center. Still no apple is removed. Repeat another two sets of crossed double cuts, placing them equidistant between the other crossed cuts. As you make this second series of double cuts, the ends of the cuts will begin intersecting with each other. When this happens, small wedges of apple will begin to fall out.

This garnish should be cut the day it is used. Wrap it in plastic wrap or immerse it in cold water and refrigerate it (depending upon which fruit or vegetable you use) until ready for use. If you use an apple or a mushroom, brush the finished flower with lemon juice to prevent it from turning brown.

The resulting piece serves as an attractive centerpiece for a large platter or as part of a small grouping of flowers.

You can make this flower with a radish, a mushroom, cucumber ends, an apple, a lemon, or a melon (especially cantaloupe). You can create a similar design simply by cutting a series of eight

wedges connected at one central point, but this
reverse or inverted technique gives the flower a more
coordinated rhythm.

Eggplant Daisy

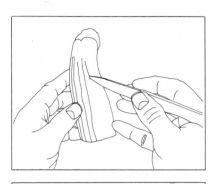

Japanese eggplants are a bit smaller than the large bulbous ones we are accustomed to. Both have the same purple skin, but the Japanese variety is generally a shade lighter. They run 6 to 8 inches in length and 1 to 2 inches in diameter. For this flower, choose a firm, unblemished Japanese eggplant. From the fatter end, cut away a piece about 1 inch long and discard it. Grasp the remaining piece in your free hand, with the narrower part pointing upward. Holding a paring knife in your other hand, make a series of parallel scores in the purple skin, roughly ¼ inch apart, all around the eggplant. These scores should extend from within 1 inch of the untrimmed end, back down to the opposite, cut end.

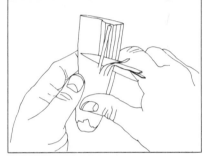

Invert the eggplant. Insert the tip of the paring knife between the skin and the flesh, going under the skin enough to reach across to the adjacent score. Using a back-and-forth sawing motion, separate the ¼-inch-wide strip of skin form the underlying flesh as far down as the score. Repeat this procedure all the way around the eggplant until all the petals are curving outward. The remaining center piece of eggplant, from which the strips of skin were removed, can now be severed at its base and discarded.

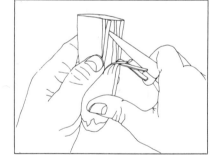

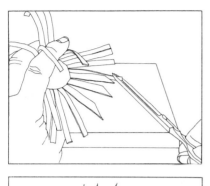

With a pair of scissors, trim each squared petal end to a point. This trimming adds finesse to the finished flower.

When the flower is completed, immerse it immediately in water that is slightly acidulated with fresh lemon juice. It will keep for a day.

This garnish should be made the same day it is to be served.

The eggplant daisy is an excellent addition to a flower garnish and is also appropriate for any baked eggplant dish, such as moussaka.

Part III | SOCLES AND COLLARS

Baskets

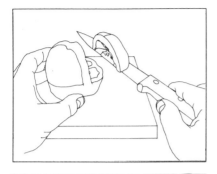

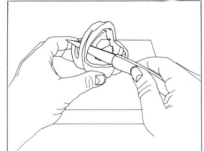

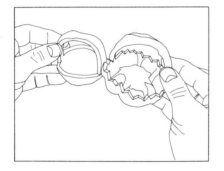

A socle is any container fashioned out of food and used as a base or pedestal to hold another food item. It adds a decorative touch to the simplest buffet.

Baskets are one form of socle, and they are easy to create. Bell peppers and citrus fruits make ideal baskets. A pepper is particularly good because of its hollow interior.

Stand a fresh, unblemished pepper (green, yellow, or red) upright on a cutting board. If the bottom is uneven and the pepper rocks slightly, cut a paper-thin slice from the bottom so that it sits securely on the board. Using a paring knife, make two vertical incisions down from the top, leaving a ¼-inch-wide strip of pepper between the cuts. Now make two horizontal cuts perpendicular to the vertical ones and on opposite sides of the pepper. Remove the two upper quarters of the pepper. The ¼-inch-wide piece will remain as the handle of the basket.

Carefully remove the inner connecting tissue inside the pepper, as well as the seeds. If you wish, you can cut a zigzag pattern around the edge of the basket or the edge of the handle after you have completed the basket.

If immersed in cold water and refrigerated, a pepper basket will keep for two days. Change the water daily.

This basket can now be served hot or cold, filled with such items as carrots Parisienne, corn relish, creamed onions, or an herbed mayonnaise.

Baskets are very versatile and can also be made from lemons, oranges, grapefruits, melons, and the ends of cucumbers.

Lattice Squash Collars

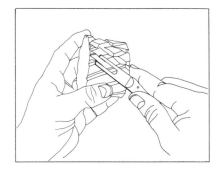

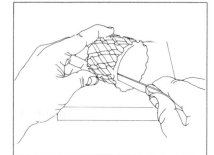

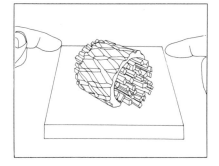

This socle variation came about when I was developing a vegetable pâté platter for entry in the 1983 New York Culinary Salon Food Show.

Cut a 3-inch-long cylindrical segment from the center of a butternut squash. (Any similar squash is good for this technique.) Do not peel it. Scoop out the center of the squash, using a paring knife and a Parisienne scoop. The walls of the hollowed-out cylinder should be roughly ⅜ inch thick.

With a channel knife, cut a lattice design into the outside surface of the squash. To make a slanted pattern, cut parallel channels at approximately a 30-degree angle from the vertical, roughly ½ inch apart. Each channel should run the full length of the cylinder. Make a second set of parallel channels at a 30-degree angle from the vertical and perpendicular to the first set of channels. You now have a lattice design.

Blanch the squash collar by plunging it into boiling salted water for 3 to 4 minutes. It must remain firm. Remove the squash, drain, and pat dry.

You can now tip the collar on its side and fill the inside space with julienned garden vegetables—string beans, carrots, celery, or zucchini.

You can set up this item in advance, blanching the collar and the julienned vegetables to *al dente* and assembling them. Then do the last few minutes of cooking and heating in a steamer. Or immerse the collar and vegetables in simmering lightly salted water. Drizzle with melted butter just before serving.

Cut the collar no earlier than a day before it is used. Immerse it in cold water and refrigerate it until ready for blanching.

Cucumber Timbale

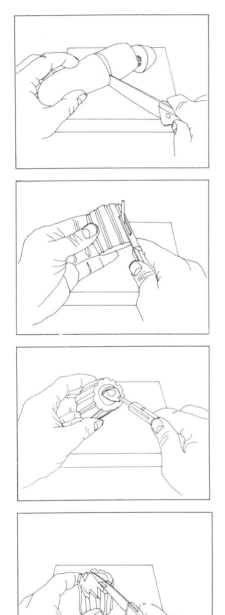

Timbale comes from a French word for *drum*.
Originally connoting a small beverage cup, the
timbale now has a much broader meaning. Small cups
of different shapes are used as molds for all kinds of
forcemeats, vegetable side dishes, and aspic.

With a utility knife, cut one end off a large,
unpeeled cucumber and then cut a 2½- to 3-inch-long
segment. Using a channel knife, carve a pattern
around the outside of the timbale. The pattern can be
as simple as parallel vertical channels, ⅜ inch apart,
or as elaborate as a crisscrossed diagonal lattice design
(see photo in the color section).

Remove the insides of the timbale with a Parisienne
scoop, leaving about ½ inch of the vegetable bottom
intact. The sides should remain ¼ inch thick.

Use a paring knife to cut a pattern around the top
edge of the timbale. A small zigzag cut will suffice, or
small rounded domes, pared into shape with the tip of
the knife and spaced as far apart as the exterior
vertical or lattice channels.

Once cut, this timbale will keep for nearly three
days if immersed in cold water and refrigerated.
Change the water daily.

Use this item to hold individual sauces—a warm
sauce such as hollandaise or bearnaise or a cold sauce
or dip such as herbed mayonnaise, tartar sauce, or
yogurt dip.

Although this piece is usually fashioned from a
cucumber, it can also be made with any squash such
as zucchini or summer squash.

Multipetaled Cucumber Timbale

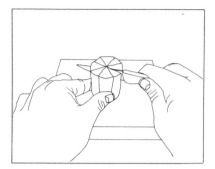

With a utility knife, cut one end off an unpeeled cucumber. Then cut a 2-inch-long segment and stand it, flat side up, on a cutting board.

Using a paring knife, make four 1½-inch-deep incisions into the top of the segment. Each incision should run completely across the top so that there are eight equidistant segments in the circle.

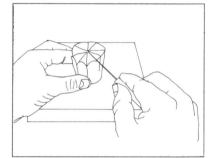

Taper the eight sections with the paring knife, trimming them into elongated domes. Using the tip of the paring knife, carefully separate the peel from each dome. In each dome, make two or three additional incisions, parallel to the separated peel and in toward the center of the segment. (Keep the incisions close together and closer to the peel than to the center, since you will be removing the center flesh.) You should now have three or four thin petals in each of the eight domed sections.

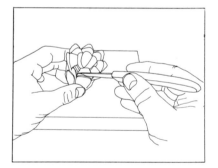

With a Parisienne scoop, remove the remaining flesh and seeds from the center, leaving a ½-inch-thick bottom.

Immerse the timbale in cold water and refrigerate. The petals will curl outward after the first twelve hours of immersion, and the timbale will keep for two days. Change the water daily.

Use the timbale as a sauce vessel or a single garnish.

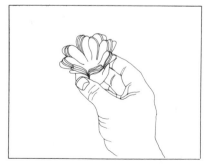

Knotted Scallion Leaf

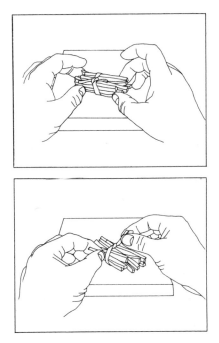

Professional chefs and cooks often use the long green leaves of scallions as edible cord or twine. This is a tidy and colorful way to present a vegetable *du jour*.

To soften the scallion leaves so that they are flexible enough to tie into knots, drop them into lightly sugared water for 10 to 15 seconds. (Use 1 tablespoon of sugar per gallon of water. This intensifies and retains the green color.)

To tie up a bundle of julienned vegetables, make a simple square knot by tying two consecutive overhand knots. The first overhand knot (the same as the first step in tying a pair of shoelaces) should be taut enough to hold the small bundle together, but do not pull it so tight that the leaf snaps. Tie a second overhand knot above this, making it taut enough to secure the whole thing. Snip away any remaining ends with a scissors. (For extra-long bundles, such as asparagus, you can make two or three such ties.)

Use these leaves to tie up a bundle of asparagus, fresh string beans, or julienned carrots, squash, or potatoes. Blanch the vegetables *al dente* before you tie them together. When you are ready to serve the dish, plunge the entire bundle into lightly salted and buttered boiling water for 15 or 20 seconds. Remove and drain.

The scallion leaves should be blanched the same day as their intended use; if stored for a day, they soften and begin to lose some of their color.

Carrot Ring

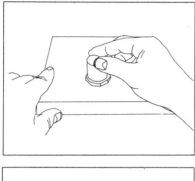

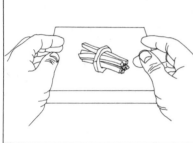

Peel a fat carrot and use a utility knife to remove a ¼-inch-thick slice from the thicker end. Place the slice on a cutting board.

Select a circle cutter that has a diameter roughly ¼ inch smaller than the diameter of the slice. Position the cutter over the center of the slice, push down, and remove the center circle.

Precut, raw carrot rings can be kept for four days if immersed in cold water and refrigerated. Change the water daily. To serve the garnish, blanch the carrot ring in lightly salted boiling water for about two minutes.

Use this ring as a collar to hold a small bundle of vegetables, such as asparagus, fresh string beans, or julienned carrots, squash, or potatoes. Blanch the julienned vegetables *al dente* before you put them in the collar. Then, just before serving, plunge the entire bundle into lightly salted and buttered boiling water for 15 or 20 seconds. Remove and drain.

You can also make such rings from zucchini, yellow, or butternut squash.

Part IV | DECORATIVE PIECES

Cucumber Boat

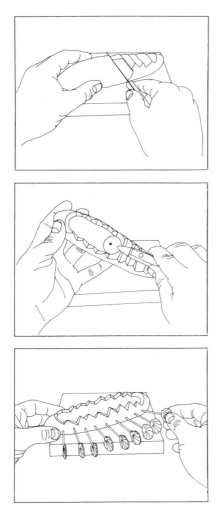

Generally I stay away from such embellishments as hard-boiled-egg frogs, carrot palm trees, and acorn squash carts, but this mock outrigger has a certain elegance that inspires me to use it on occasion. The cucumber boat, used with a few radish mushrooms (page 34), lends an exotic feeling to any platter of Asian cuisine.

Choose a broad, nicely curved, unblemished cucumber. (The larger and more interestingly curved cucumber you select, the larger and more interesting the boat.) Remove any oil or wax coating by washing the cucumber in tepid water with Ivory soap, Dr. Bronner's peppermint soap, or some other natural soap. Place it horizontally on a cutting board.

With a paring knife, remove the top third of the cucumber by cutting a zigzag down the length of the vegetable. Add a slight downward curve as you start each zigzag and a slight upward curve as you finish it. Remove each loose wedge as you go along. With a Parisienne scoop or a sharp-edged teaspoon, remove all of the seeds and pulp.

Along one side of the boat, insert up to a dozen paddle-ended toothpicks, which have a flat fan shape on one end and double tines on the other end. I have also used plastic bar stirrers for this purpose—the kind that have a small, square plaque at one end advertising the name of a bar. These make excellent oars. Whichever props you decide to use for oars, they should be secured into only one side of the boat, fanning slightly outward.

Make the cucumber boat the day it is used. Store it for no longer than a day—on a small plate, covered with plastic wrap, and refrigerated.

When you are ready to serve this piece, place the boat on a platter, allowing it to lean and rest on the row of oars. Then you can fill the cavity with an appropriate accompaniment to a main dish—chutney, a hot or cold savory sauce, Greek olives, or poached prawns.

Looped Lemon I

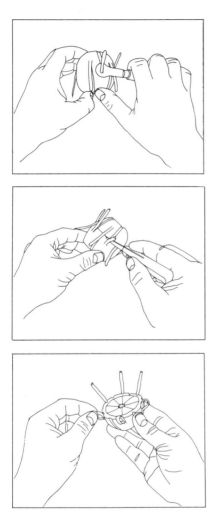

This garnish reminds me of some of the very elaborate engravings in late-nineteenth-century cookbooks, such as *The Epicurean,* an enormous volume by Charles Ranhofer, a chef at New York's Delmonico's, and *Le Livre de Cuisine,* by Jules Gouffé, a disciple of Antonin Carême, one of the founders of classic French cooking. These engravings often are more elaborate than the real thing.

With a utility knife, slice off both ends of a large, blemish-free lemon, just enough to flatten them. Hold the lemon in one hand, and with a channel knife, cut a strip of peel down from the edge of one of the cut-off ends. Continue this strip or channel down the lemon, stopping ½ inch from the opposite end, where it remains attached to the lemon. (This strip must be thick enough so that it will not break later when it is looped.)

Carefully pull the channel knife all the way up until it comes off the separated strip of peel. Repeat the procedure, making parallel strips all the way around the lemon. Start from the same end each time and make the strips ¾ inch apart. There will be eight to ten strips in all, depending upon the diameter of the lemon.

Invert the lemon and repeat the procedure, locating this second series of strips between pairs of strips made from the opposite direction. By making two sets of strips that go in opposite directions, you can be economical and produce two garnishes per lemon.

With a paring knife, cut the lemon exactly in half across its width (parallel to the cut ends). Be careful not to sever any of the loose strips. Now take one lemon half and loop each dangling strip by turning it inward and gently inserting the outside end of each strip into its own base. The outward pressure of each loop, jammed gently into that tight space between the base of the strip and the rest of the lemon, will hold the strip in place. Repeat this procedure with all of the strips. If some of the loops pop out, reinsert them until they stay in place.

Assemble this garnish the same day it is served. You

can put completed lemons on a small plate, cover them with plastic wrap, and refrigerate them until ready for use.

This makes an excellent plate or platter garnish for seafood or any dish that includes lemon in its ingredients.

Looped Lemon II

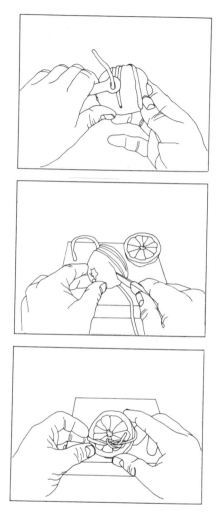

Strips of lemon peel can be used to create other garnishes besides those shown in *Looped Lemon I* (page 76).

With a utility knife, slice off both ends of a large, blemish-free lemon, just enough to flatten them. Hold the lemon in one hand, and, with a channel knife, cut a strip of peel about three-fourths around the widest center section of the lemon. Slide the channel knife back off the full length of this strip, being careful not to crack or break it. Next, make two parallel incisions across the width of the lemon. These parallel slices should run adjacent to the two sides of the previously cut channel. (Be careful not to sever the loose lemon strip.) This will produce a lemon slice roughly ¼ inch thick, with three-fourths of the peel separated as a long strip.

Tie one or two simple overhand knots into the strip. (An overhand knot is the same loop used in the first step of tying a shoelace.) Do not pull the knot too taut, or the peel may break.

A variation of this piece can be created by cutting two channels in opposite directions, each one covering half of the center circumference of the lemon. Remove a ¼-inch-thick slice from the center of the lemon by making two parallel incisions: one across the width of the lemon, the other adjacent to the two sides of the double strip just channeled. After the slice is removed, tie the two strips in a square knot across the face of the lemon. (A square knot is two consecutive overhand knots. First knot: place right end over left end; pull through. Second knot: place left end over right end; pull through.) Again, do not pull the ends too tightly or the strips may break.

Prepare this garnish the same day it will be served. Cover the garnish in plastic wrap and refrigerate it until ready for use.

Lemon garnishes are appropriate in many dishes, including almost any prepared fish. They may also be used with chicken or tuna salads, stuffed tomato, or floated in a finger bowl.

Celery Sea Anemone

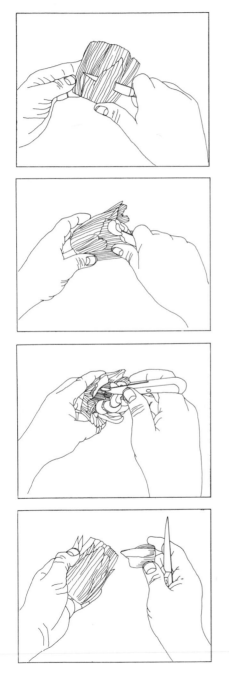

This unusual flower is an innovation of mine, inspired by watching hundreds of celery bottoms being tossed into the nearest stockpot. I have always thought they could be put to better use.

With a utility knife, remove a 3- to 3½-inch segment from the bottom of a stalk of celery by making a clean incision through the bunch, perpendicular to its length. (Use the longer portions of the loose celery ribs in a soup or salad, as a vegetable, or as a sauce garnish.)

With a paring knife, cut a slice no more than ¼ inch thick from the bottom of that 3-inch-long segment, to remove the soiled end.

Hold the remaining celery "butt" upright in one hand. There will be roughly five outer ribs, which should spiral around, encircling some smaller ribs of celery.

On the outside of one of these five outer ribs, use the paring knife to cut a thin petal, beginning one-third of the way down from the top of the rib and stopping just under 1 inch from the bottom. To the left and right of this petal, cut two other petals in the same manner, one on each side. These outer ribs are wide enough to have room for three petal slices each. Repeat this procedure on the other four outer ribs.

On the top of the circle of remaining smaller interior ribs, take the top of the knife and shave the outer edge of that inner circle so that it slopes down and out from the center to the periphery. What should remain is the central dome, surrounded by the elevated circle of outer celery ribs (the part left over when you started cutting the petals one-third of the way down each rib).

Hold the paring knife so that it points directly downward toward the core. Working only on the interior ribs, make incisions straight down through each rib, going as far as possible without weakening the structure of the flower. Repeat this technique over and over, making parallel incisions roughly ⅛ inch apart. Because of the proximity of these incisions, if they are not parallel, they may intersect at the base,

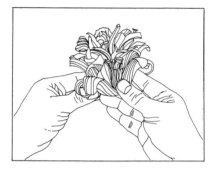

severing some of the slender pieces being cut.

With the top center pared away into a dome shape, and more than a dozen petals cut into the sides of the outer ribs, there still should be a rather blunt-looking piece of each outer rib elevated slightly above the outer edge of the center dome. Remove this upper portion of each outer rib by reinserting the paring knife into the outside petal cuts and working the knife down in until that chunk can be removed.

Immerse the flower in cold water and refrigerate. Overnight, the outer and inner petals will all curve elaborately, spreading the flower outward and crisping those shapes into permanent positions. Since there is no way to control this process, there is also no way to anticipate what shapes and patterns will result. Whatever shapes it does adopt, however, it will have the look of a water-tossed sea anemone.

This garnish will keep well for up to a week if immersed in cold water and refrigerated. Change the water daily.

Use the sea anemone as a centerpiece on a platter of roasts, surrounded with tomato roses (page **25**), or on a large platter of marinated vegetables and other antipastos.

Cabbage Blossom

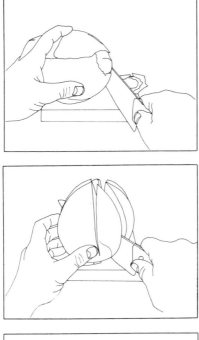

I discovered this rather impressive garnish quite by accident when I was trying to find a way to use a large vegetable to fill space on a huge table display of raw vegetables. As an experiment, I cut a head of cabbage into eight wedges, keeping everything attached at the core, and dropped it into a 5-gallon bucket of cold water. The next day, to my surprise, the entire head had opened up into a huge and magnificent eight-petaled flower.

Choose a red or white cabbage of whatever size you desire. Remove the loose outer leaves. Using an 8- or 10-inch French knife, slice the cabbage along the bottom core, just enough to allow the vegetable to have a flattened bottom. Place the cabbage on its bottom on a cutting board.

You will be cutting the wedges straight across through an imaginary center point. Make the first incision perpendicular to the board, straight down through the cabbage to about 1 inch from the bottom. Make a second incision exactly perpendicular to the first cut, again down to 1 inch above the core. This will make four equal wedges. Make two more incisions in the same way, thus dividing the four wedges into eight equidistant ones.

Immerse the cabbage in a large container of cold water and refrigerate. (The container must be large enough to allow the flower to expand to nearly double the width of the original cabbage.) After the flower has opened completely, the cold water will crisp it and keep its shape.

The cabbage will keep well for up to a week if immersed in cold water and refrigerated. Change the water daily.

Use the cabbage blossom for a buffet or table embellishment, or as part of a centerpiece bouquet.

Because brussels sprouts are members of the cabbage family, you can use this same technique on them.

Apple Dove and Rococo Apple

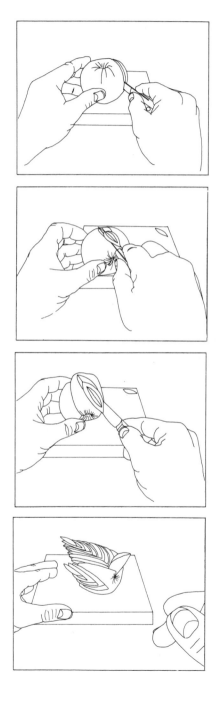

The apple dove is a magnificent piece that looks very complex and is somewhat difficult to describe, but essentially it involves a very simple technique. With a little practice, a modicum of patience, and an ever-sharp paring knife, it is not too difficult to execute.

Begin by placing a firm red apple on a cutting board, its stem facing upward. At an angle perpendicular to the board, cut a slice off any side of the apple. (Use a paring knife for this.) The slice should be ½ inch at its thickest point. Set the slice aside for later use.

Turn the apple so it rests on its cut surface. The stem end of the apple (the top) should be facing you, with the core perpendicular to your chest. Beginning at the top center, make a series of V cuts, each one running in the same direction as the core. Start with a tiny V no deeper than ¼ inch. (The angles of each V should be roughly 50 to 55 degrees.) Make each of the first two incisions for that first wedge only as deep as necessary for them to intersect so that the wedge separates. Take out the wedge, dip it in lemon juice, and set it off to one side. An open V groove will remain. Now continue cutting consecutive Vs all the way down into the apple, each one beneath the one removed, until you cut into the core.

The thickness of each consecutive wedge depends on you. The more finely you cut them, the more elaborate and delicate the finished dove will look. An Asian student in one of my food-sculpture classes cut these wedges ¹⁄₁₆ inch thick. You do not need to cut them that thin, but they should be in the vicinity of ⅛ inch.

Remove each wedge as it is cut and dip it in lemon juice. Line up all the wedges consecutively to one side. When you are first beginning to work with this technique, it is very important to line up the wedges in the order they were cut.

The bottom of the last wedge extends into the core of the apple. After you have removed it and dipped it in lemon juice, reassemble all of the wedges in the order they were cut and set the assembly aside.

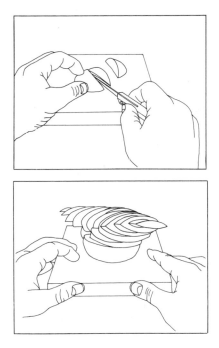

Now turn the apple 90 degrees and cut four or five of the same kind of consecutive wedges in the side facing you. Since these wedges will become wings for the dove, they should be angled slightly upward, toward what will become the tail of the bird. (The stem top of the apple will become the breast of the bird, the opposite end will become the tail.)

Remove each of these wedges, dip them in lemon juice, and line them up. When you have cut four or five wedges, reassemble them and set the whole piece aside. Turn the apple around and make a second set of side wedges, again angled slightly upward toward the tail of the bird.

After you have cut the three sets of wedges, dipped all parts in lemon juice, and reassembled them in the order they were cut, replace each set in the apple, the body of the bird. The moistness of the apple and its sugar content provide enough adhesive to hold together all of the cut parts.

With the point of the paring knife, or with your fingertips, gently slide each of the top wedges toward the bottom of the apple (the tail of the bird). Slide each wedge about ⅛ to ¼ inch beyond the one beneath it. Repeat this procedure with the two sets of side wedges.

There are many different ways to fashion the bird's head, but the following technique probably is the easiest. Place the original apple slice (the one you set aside) flat side down on the cutting board in front of you. From the center of this slice, cut a wedge that is ¼ inch wide on the skin side. (This wedge should be as long as the slice itself.) Dip it in lemon juice. This will be the bird's head.

With the paring knife, gouge out a tiny hole at the point of the innermost center wedge, right at the breast of the bird. Take the wedge for the head and push one end of it, its flesh part facing outward, into the tiny hole. (If it fails to stay in place, try enlarging the hole a bit. As an extreme measure, you can use a toothpick to secure the head in place at the point where it sits in the hole.) I prefer to leave the bird without eyes, lending a mystical air to it, but if you wish to add eyes, insert two whole cloves in the head where eyes would be.

The rococo apple, my own variation of the apple dove, is a sort of art deco sculptured form. Given its dramatic appearance, it is always received with great excitement.

Begin by cutting and discarding (or eating) a ¾-inch-thick slice from the side of a firm red apple. Turn the apple so it rests on a cutting board on this cut surface.

Now, *visually* mark two upper quarters in the apple. These two upper quarters are in the same position as if you were to cut the apple horizontally right through its center and then cut that half into two equal halves. But do not cut anything yet. The outside edges of these two visually marked quarters will be the outermost boundaries of two sets of consecutively cut wedges.

The technique is the same as that for the dove, except that the angle of the wedges for this piece should be exactly 90 degrees, so that each wedge has one horizontal side and one vertical side. There should be approximately five to seven wedges in each of the two top apple quarters, depending on the size of the apple and the thickness of the wedges. As with the dove, dip each removed wedge in lemon juice, then reassemble the wedges in the apple. Spread out the finished wedges by pushing the two sets of wedges away from each other in opposite directions.

Even with the lemon-juice bath, an apple soon will begin to turn brown once it is exposed to air. Thus, these pieces should be made no earlier than a half day before they are used. If you use liberal amounts of lemon juice and slide out the wedges close to the time of use, the pieces will keep for a half day if covered tightly with plastic wrap and refrigerated.

I generally use these garnishes to accompany a dessert service of fruit and cheese.

With practice, you can develop the dexterity to

make these garnishes just before they are needed. When you have reached such a degree of dexterity with this technique, you do not have to remove the individual wedges. You cut each wedge, making sure that it is fully separated, and then cut the next one. You can thus eliminate the lemon-juice bath and the wedge lineup. Just squeeze half of a lemon over the finished garnish just before it is used.

Another option with this technique is the apple feather. Cut an apple into quarters and remove the core on each quarter by slicing it off, leaving a flat base on which the quarter rests. You can then cut each quarter into a feather by employing the same wedge-cutting technique used for the dove and the rococo apple. It will resemble a larger version of the radish feather (page 37).

Tomato Wing

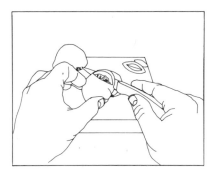

This is a variation on the radish feather (page **37**) and the apple dove and rococo apple (page **82**).

Begin by halving a large, ripe, red tomato along its core with a paring knife. Turn the tomato so the cut surface lies flat on a cutting board. Make a series of consecutive **V**-shaped wedges in the upper surface of a tomato half. Make one beneath the other, removing each one as you go and lining them up in order. When you have cut six or more wedges, reassemble them and put the piece aside.

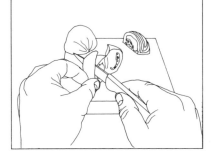

Turn the tomato half bottom-side-up. Slip the paring knife underneath the skin at the center top, and, sawing back and forth with the paring knife, remove a ¹⁄₁₆-inch-thick layer of skin, down to within ½ inch of the bottom. With the tomato still inverted, repeat this procedure on the opposite side.

When you are ready to use this garnish, slide the center wedges toward the rear and push out both of the side slices. It should look rather like a bird without a head.

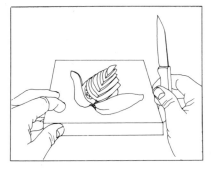

This garnish must be prepared the same day it will be used. It can be made early in the day, covered tightly with plastic wrap, and refrigerated.

Staircase

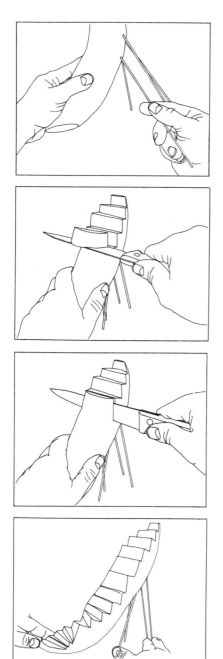

I have a lot of fun with this piece, and I often incorporate it into my *mukimono* bouquets to lend them the feeling of a tropical lagoon. Sometimes I prop up the staircase with 8-inch-long bamboo skewers and use it as a platter garnish, surrounded at its base by vegetable flowers.

You can use any crisp, elongated vegetable for this, including zucchini, yellow squash, English cucumber, and daikon (Japanese white radish). Daikon is especially good because it is wide and long and is often crooked. Variations in shape are welcome here, since they allow you to create interesting curves in a staircase.

Begin by positioning the vegetable at a 65- to 70-degree angle. Then slice off the bottom of the vegetable, exactly parallel to the horizontal plane, allowing the vegetable to sit flat while in that angled position. Insert two or three 8-inch-long bamboo skewers into the upper part, extending straight down, to prop up the vegetable while you work.

Using a French knife, start at the top with a vertical cut about 1 inch deep. Intersect that with a horizontal cut, thus separating a small section from the vegetable. Repeat this all the way down to the other end of the vegetable, curving the direction of the stairs back and forth by varying the horizontal plane of each vertical cut.

A daikon staircase will keep for a week if immersed in cold water and refrigerated. Cucumbers will keep for a day or two if immersed in cold water and refrigerated. Zucchini will last for up to three days if treated the same way. Change the water for all types daily.

Looped Orange Wedges

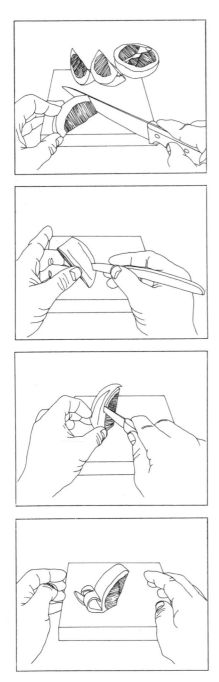

Begin by using a French knife to cut a ripe navel orange into eight wedges around its core. One at a time, lay each wedge on a cutting board, cut side down, and remove the point from one end. This cut must be exactly perpendicular to the wedge itself so that it will stand upright. Trim until each wedge can do this.

With a paring knife held like a pencil, score a V shape through the skin on a wedge. The score should be no deeper than ¼ inch.

Carefully separate a thin layer of the skin from the back of the wedge. (This can be a bit difficult and time-consuming because of the contour of the orange.) The best way to approach this is to cut from both sides. The skin must be thin enough so that it will bend without breaking. Make this cut from the top of the wedge down to within ½ inch of the bottom. Curl this partly severed slice of skin inward and down. Keep pushing the loop down into its own base until it stays there. The scored V shape in the center of the skin will stick up and out, producing an interesting effect on the finished piece.

This garnish should be made the same day it is served. If necessary, it can be stored for several hours, covered tightly with plastic wrap and refrigerated.

I use this garnish by lining up looped orange wedges in curved rows on a platter with other fruits, perhaps with a selection of appropriate cheeses.

This technique also works well with apples and grapefruit.

Alternated Pineapple Wedges

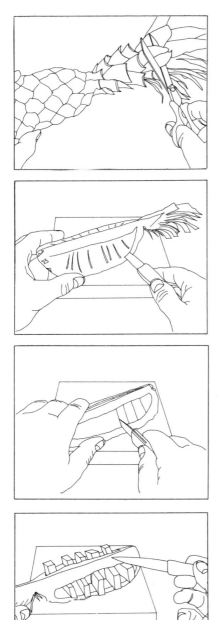

Choose a pineapple that appears to be ripe. With a scissors, remove the brown and unattractive ends of the leaves. Rinse the pineapple in cold water, drain, and dry.

Using a French knife, split the pineapple into four equal quarters. Leave the greenery intact on each wedge.

The lengthwise top edge of each wedge, the center of the original pineapple, is woody and inedible, so this will remain intact. About ½ inch below the top of this woody part, insert a paring knife and slide it the full length of the wedge. Continue this cut down and around, encircling the inner edible part of the fruit. Leave roughly a ¼-inch-thick shell all around. (When making this incision, work the paring knife in from both sides of the wedge to compensate for its curvature.)

When the inner section of fruit is fully separated and still inside its shell, make a series of vertical incisions through this edible part, from ¼ to ½ inch apart, making sure that the slices are completely loosened from the shell. Push out these slices alternately to each side.

This garnish must be prepared the same day it is used. Serve it well chilled. It is a nice touch to present it on an abundant bed of crushed ice.

INDEX